Drawing the Crow

Adrian Mitchell has taught and written about Australian literature for many years. Born in Adelaide, he worked as a lecturer there before moving to Sydney, where he became Head of the School of English, Art History, Film and Media at the University of Sydney. His next book is about the buccaneer and navigator, William Dampier.

Drawing the Crow

Adrian Mitchell

Wakefield
Press

Wakefield Press
1 The Parade West
Kent Town
South Australia 5067
www.wakefieldpress.com.au

First published 2006
Reprinted 2006
Copyright © Adrian Mitchell, 2006

Cover and text designed by Liz Nicholson, designBITE
Typeset by Ryan Paine, Wakefield Press
Printed and bound by Hyde Park Press

National Library of Australia
Cataloguing-in-publication entry

Mitchell, Adrian, 1941– .
Drawing the crow.

ISBN 1 86254 685 1.

1. South Australia – Social life and customs.
2. South Australia – History. I. Title.

994.23

Publication of this book was assisted
by the Commonwealth Government
through the Australia Council,
its arts funding and advisory body.

Government
of South Australia

Arts SA

Australia Council
for the Arts

fox creek

Contents

Foreword

Sue Woolfe

I'm never to be a young man, and I've visited Adelaide only twice. Yet Adelaide-born Adrian Mitchell creates such empathy that with this book for company, I swim a mile-wide river though I'm a one-length puffer at the local baths, I'm terrorised by the strangling hands of a cousin at night, I watch a sea-obsessed woman prise meat out of periwinkles with her hairpin, I discover I share the mysterious gift of the local water-diviner. I'm gormless but hoping no one will notice, I'm finding that the foreign city of Sydney demands social skills I didn't know I lacked, I discover that as a young man I'm no longer comfortably a spectator, I have to relocate, with pain, hilarity and humiliation, the self. This is because Mitchell's panoply of characters including himself as narrator, whether they delight, amuse or appall, all engage me in the way that the creations of the best novelists do.

But the characters are not fiction, they're real-life people from Mitchell's poignant, wry, vivacious memories of the passage between adolescence and manhood in his home country. As he explores its boundaries, he questions what those boundaries mean to him – do they enclose or liberate or something in between? – and he peers into what lies beyond them. In his unflinching honesty, he allows himself, and us, to be baffled, astounded, demolished and in the end, to some extent, made a little wiser.

In a way this book gave me what the best travel does. I found myself following wherever this writer wanted to lead. His memories and his musing upon them acted as a benign electric shock to my own imprecise, almost forgotten memories. I wanted him to keep talking long after I closed the book, because he'd made my own past more precious, more actual.

Author's Note

These essays are not intended to be autobiographical, though of course what they tell is inevitably tethered to me. They are not about who I was, but where I came from. It is axiomatic that nothing happened in Adelaide in the comfortably apolitical years of the Playford era, and these essays testify to that. There was just nothing much to write home about; and we hadn't gone anywhere anyway. These essays attempt to represent a South Australian point of view, or something like a set of South Australian eyes, to put down on paper (injudicious phrase) how it was for us, growing up through the fifties, and extending into the years before and after that decade, in a perfectly ordinary home in a perfectly ordinary suburb, and rediscovering the richness of it.

Would we have wanted it any different? That is an un-South Australian question. We were brought up to accept what we had. Each meal at home began with grace: '. . . the Lord make us truly grateful'. And then, if we appeared not to like the look of it, our mother would add, 'Eat up your missionary'.

Early versions of three of the first four essays appeared some years ago in *Quadrant*, which may explain their particular cast. A modified version of the second essay was presented at a conference in Trevendrum, India, in 2004, and in time will be published in the collected proceedings. Others have sat in inchoate form in folders and the backs of drawers; and of course, in even more inchoate form in the corners of my mind. If they appear somewhat of a jumble, very well, I am not Walt Whitman.

Drawing the crow? G.A.Wilkes (*A Dictionary of Australian Colloquialisms*) explains the other meaning of the phrase as 'to come off worst in any allocation'. It is not quite the same as drawing the short straw, or having Buckley's. But it is better than a poke in the eye with a blunt stick; probably.

1

Knowing Your Place

A Short View of South Australia

In South Australia I was born,
Heave away! haul away!
In South Australia, round Cape Horn,
We're bound for South Australia.

If memory serves, that sea-shanty was discovered in Nova
Scotia. Why it should have survived there invites conjecture;
it reminds those who have neglected their history, or possibly
never encountered it, that the great wool-clippers (sailing
ships, not shearing blades) and grain carriers as well as the
coastal trade must have supported a wealth of song and folk-
lore, now dispersed across the seven seas. To those sensitive
to even more momentary frissons, it seems entirely characteristic that South Australia should find its self-reference
somewhere else.

And that is just the kind of remark to put South Australia
in its place – as distinct from allowing South Australia to say
what it thinks its place is. It is the kind of remark that doesn't
identify anything about South Australia; rather, it identifies
an attitude external to it. It is the sort of careless dismissive-
ness that has devised the nickname 'croweater', unkindest of
the various state monikers – though the Western Australia

1

'sandgroper' is not a whole lot more flattering. Adelaide, the wags used to say, was laid out in 1836 and never got up again. Wags being wags, no doubt they are still saying it.

From within the state's cultural borders, though, and more particularly in Adelaide where I grew up, the customary estimations take on a different orientation, and what may appear ironic to others is perfectly straightforward to the locals, or ironic for different reasons. At one time, in the earliest days of the Festival of the Arts, there was an attempt to promote Adelaide as 'Queen City of the South', but that made us uncomfortable, too ostentatious by far. In any case it was not clear what we were being set up against, which Queen City of the North we were being measured against. Yet we could acknowledge the playful promotional spin of the label. The other, older tag, 'City of Churches', identifies not a freak of architecture nor a rampaging wowserism, either current or in the past, but a lifestyle of civic steadiness, regularity and propriety, the values of its founding settlement, in both its English and German constituency.

What South Australians have done, perhaps more doggedly than those in any other region, is to veil or reserve their own regional identity – not because of any sense of inadequacy or unfitness, but because that is the peculiar character of the South Australian. They have no sense of disjunction or aloofness or separateness from that more billowy eiderdown, the national character. But the terms by which South Australia snuggles in with the other states may be misconstrued. For example, South Australian schoolchildren have for generations responded to the collective fervours of nationalism. We were encouraged to embrace Clancy of the Overflow and the Man from Snowy River as our own, we plunged with Henry Kendall down the soggy gullies in pursuit of something called the bell-bird, with just the same anticipation as if it had been a nightingale. What is a bell-bird to a South Australian schoolchild? Who can say? Something in a poem, is what. Outside our range of experience. What kind of mountains were these where there are rampaging brumby musters? Ditto. From a South Australian perspective, Australian poetry and Australian cultural icons are no more and no less real than English poetry and English cultural icons. They have the same 'authenticity'. That is, they are equally remote, equally distant, equally an acquired mantle. This is not to say that Australia is to South Australia as England is to Australia. For South Australia, the concepts of England and Australia are similarly endorsed yet similarly external.

When the colonies began meeting to discuss federation, the South Australian role was to ensure that it was not disadvantaged by New South Wales. This might still be recognised as a sensible precaution, but South Australia was in area a very considerable colony, for its jurisdiction included (1862–1911) what is now known as the Northern Territory, and perhaps that gave the delegates an unusual sense of themselves. Manning Clark called them 'conditional converts', yet in the community itself the question of national formation was already settled. As early as 1859, the South Australian poetess Caroline Carleton had composed an anthem, 'The Song of Australia':

> *There is a land where summer skies*
> *Are gleaming with a thousand dyes*
> *Blending in witching harmonies;*
> *And grassy knoll and forest height*
> *Are flushing in the rosy light,*
> *And all above is azure bright –*
> *Australia!*

The patriotism in that song was comprehensive and effusive. It became not the South Australian anthem but the anthem South Australia wanted for Australia. And it sounds splendid. Clark's dismissive phrase is, incidentally, a good example of what needles South Australians. There is to the South Australian eye an unpleasant and unwarranted eastern states snootiness exposed there. What if we were to retaliate by drawing attention to the size of a head that needed a hat as big as that?

The experience of South Australia, and of being South Australian, inevitably echoes national patterns. No less importantly, however, there were and there are local differences. The essays in this book attempt to represent some of those differences, though recognising that they describe variations of what will be familiar elsewhere. Living in South Australia, and more specifically, living in Adelaide, you take on a point of view about yourself relative to the rest of Australia. You approach common experiences in a way that leaves its trace on you, shapes your perceptions. That is not to insist on uniqueness or distinctiveness. It is a point of view that is part and parcel of growing up in what may as well be thought of as the State of Grace, and which we take away with us when we leave (as so many of us, falling, have done). It is, in other words, something abiding, manifest across the experience of the past as well as in the on-going present. I have chosen to look for these traces in the fifties and sixties, the boomtime of the Playford era, when South Australia in its modern manifestation was becoming established; that is, when it was starting to part company from a much older version of its cultural life. The same sorts of observations could probably be made from more recent times; but this is my call, and this is how I remember it.

To begin with a recognisable example, while the whole

of Australia enthused about the 1954 Royal Visit, it has amused the cultural historians, mainly Easterners, to recount that South Australia enthused more than most. This was somehow quaintly in character. It is true that at a carefully chosen venue, the main racecourse, massed choirs of primary school children lifted up their voice as one – well, not quite one – and sang 'Elizabeth of England' perhaps to remind the Queen that, while she was welcome, she wasn't exactly at home here. And they sang enthusiastically of the summer skies dreaming with a thousand eyes, and so conjured up a strangely oriental notion as well as suggesting what was very likely the case, that we were all being watched. Some of us were bold enough to sing an alternative set of words:

> There is a land where all the flies
> Crawl up your nose and in your eyes ...

The fact that an established parodic version existed confirms the status of the original; but you can't find it or much else from South Australia in such regionally skewed collections as Ian Turner's *Cinderella Dressed in Yella*. When in the fullness of time 'Advance Australia Fair' won official sanction, that was tolerated in South Australia because, of course, the conferring of authority and the things authorised came from elsewhere. Privately though South Australians knew they had a better product.

Looked at carefully, 'The Song of Australia' starts to reveal some keys into its South Australian origin. There are local hints: the reference to the 'clust'ring vine' on hill and plain is apt, given that Caroline Carleton lived near Gawler, just over the hill from the Barossa Valley, while the peroration about Freedom's sons and the absence of shackl'd slaves quite pointedly allows no place for a convict. In South Australia these political ideals are actual; but that is said as matter of fact, not really of vainglory.

These things are relatively easy to see. Not so obvious is the more intimate scale of Mrs Carleton's range of reference, though a comparison with Dorothea Mackellar's 'My Country' helps to identify it. The vast sweep keeps coming back to a not-quite-identified, limited scale, of modified effusion. Treasures abound but are hidden, and so are the birds. The wealth is no longer a fabulous dream, it is real; the concealed birds do sing. For example, it has been noticed that the more moderately-coloured Adelaide rosellas are nowhere near as raucous as their gawdy cousins. Less offensive if less brilliant, perhaps. The homesteads peep from sunny plains and steep woodlands, the glad voices of children can be heard, but they are not seen – a curious antipodean reversal of that nineteenth-century ideal. The scale is domestic, unostentatious, unpretentious, and that is the kind of basis on which she proposes that the epic vision may stand. One might compare with this the quiet retirement of Charles Sturt, or a century later the reticence of Sir Douglas Mawson.

The South Australian perspective is not as in the other states or colonies. Catherine Helen Spence was at pains to express this in her first novel, *Clara Morison: A tale of South Australia during the gold fever* (1854). There, Adelaide is a tidy, self-regulating little community, but because of the Victorian goldrush many of the men are absent, and the women manage affairs until their return. The South Australian contingent went as a contingent, and brought its earnings back to Adelaide; the men distinguished themselves by their industry and good sense, and by their tendency to protection against the wilder elements on the goldfields. Spence makes it quite clear that the South Australians, while not esteeming themselves in any way as superior to the other diggers, recognise that their motives, attitudes and values differentiate them from the rest. And when they return safely to Adelaide, what Spence attends to is not any spectacular influx of wealth, but the re-establishment of a civil life complementary to the intellectual concerns of the women, who have in the meanwhile been keeping up their reading. Within a very short time they would be demanding and gaining access to the new University. And to the polling booth.

These examples from early literature confirm that South Australia was not only developing a separate sense, but began with the sense of its difference from the rest of the colonies. And whatever point one cares to make about the terms of its founding – the effect of the Wakefield system of controlled migration, the development of Torrens title, and the predominance of non-conformist values – the most powerful factor of all must surely be the positioning of South Australia in the Commonwealth. As Northrop Frye has observed of the Canadian context, so in this instance the question to consider rests on the principle that in order to find out 'Who am I?' you must discover where is here.

In anyone else's terms, South Australia isn't anywhere, it is on nobody's frame of reference. It is not one of the eastern states (the eastern bloc?), nor is it of the west; and it is not south. It certainly doesn't feel south. It feels closer to the centre, for it has a common border with all the other mainland states, but it isn't the centre. The centre is either underneath Uluru, or – in the cultural sense that carries weight – it is in the east. In either case South Australia is somewhere else. In that regard, it is like those other non-specific places, the outback, the back of beyond, the never-never, except that where they exist as a concept without a precise location, it is the concept of South Australia which appears to be up for negotiation.

The word-games that can be played indicate an important point: cultural and geographical directions undergo a re-orientation in South Australia. Or to put it yet another way, South Australia speaks another language; but its language is not yet recognised, and its terms of reference are confused because misread as well as misrepresented.

Nevertheless there is a South Australia to be read. It is there, for example, in Caroline Carleton's images of the sky, of light and brightness. More precisely, she was writing of that part of South Australia which is represented by Adelaide and its environs, but that doesn't affect the argument seriously because Adelaide and the Adelaide plains in fact represents virtually the totality. South Australia is unique in this, for that relationship is not true of any of the other state capitals. This has to do with the remarkable evenness of its landscape (persistence, some might say), its social uniformity (presumably a consequence of the Wakefield design and so on), and the lack of alternative substantial centres.

Adelaide sits in the middle of a coastal plain. The other capitals were established for their harbours, but not Adelaide. It is a plains-town, though it thinks of itself in more romantic terms as between the hills and the sea. The Adelaide plains carefully ease themselves down by St Vincent's Gulf – in spite of the name, there is nothing precipitous about being on the edge of this gulf. I suspect nobody much cares who St Vincent was, certainly not in South Australia. Good protestants pay no heed to saints, unless to the kind who sponsored the component flags of the Union Jack. Whatever the name meant to Matthew Flinders, it has acquired a local proportion. There is nothing of Abraham's bosom in this gulf, nothing of the vast profound. The gulf is flat and shallow, mostly calm. In the tranced days of summer, the gulf-dream days, it doesn't seem unreasonable to contemplate walking right across it.

In choosing imaginatively to re-situate itself that way, between the hills and the sea, Adelaide loses contact with the openness of sky and land, and finds itself cramped and confined instead. Yet that original sense of space still exists in the breadth of the streets laid down by Colonel William Light. Once there were huge gum trees across the plain, but now the remaining few of these can pretty well be individually visited. There used to be a monster Adelaide Plains gum standing at the end of Glen Osmond Road, just where the main road through the Adelaide Hills emerges; but it had to make way for quarry trucks with inadequate brakes, symbolising progress of a kind.

Another famous gum tree, the Old Gum Tree, leans on its elbow down by the beach, in a small reserve at Glenelg. It is famous because the proclamation of the state was read under its coat-hanger arch. Gum trees are naturally and whimsically grotesque, but there is nothing natural about this one. It is stuffed full of what looks like concrete and rubber, and propped up with iron rods. The proclamation may have been in effect the first tree preservation ordinance. In a curious inversion, South Australians have attached most sentimental value not to the site, nor to the historical fact of Proclamation – even though every year, in the post-Christmas heat, dignitaries of various furs and feathers gather down at the Old Gum Tree to commemorate the event – but to the survival of the tree itself. That is probably not such a bad set of priorities; in any case, it would be a mistake to write it off as endearingly provincial.

In the grotesque euphemism of early settlement, the plains were opened up, and in summer they can get warm, very warm. Adjacent to the northern fringe of the city were huge holding paddocks for livestock, and northerly winds would bring in pollen, dust-storms, flies, smoke from bush-fires and, until the sheep had quite eaten out the last of the feed, occasional plagues of locusts. The sky over Adelaide is wide open. The sun thumps you jovially between the shoulder-blades, leaps up off the footpaths and ricochets off the walls of public buildings. But it wasn't until they pulled down the overhead wires for the tramlines that you could really see Adelaide.

The day they took the wires down, back in the fifties, the plains openness was suddenly let back into the city. When the wire tracery came down in King William Street, especially the tangle of lines at the North Terrace intersection, you could start to see what Adelaide was. Until then, every street had been a kind of arcade, with awnings, verandahs and balconies down each side of the street linked by that byzantine tracery overhead – oppressive, memory says, gloomy. Dirty. But now! Pigeons, unaccustomed to the increase of light, blinked and flapped and went elsewhere. The city streets suddenly acquired their real spaciousness, and statues, until then no more than pedestrian refuges, acquired both perspective and proportion. Adelaide stood revealed, as it always had been, a city of light. On the other hand, what also stood revealed was the true brutality of the stobie poles.

For a decade or two, from the late fifties, through the sixties and into the early seventies, the Colonel's vision was manifest. It remained until the streetscapes, admirable in relation to buildings of mostly only two or three storeys, were overthrown by development. Big buildings changed the scale once more, to create in effect narrow channels of coolness (Henry Kendall again?) and threw deep shadows across the thoroughfares. Yet the idea and the meaning of

Adelaide can still be readily appreciated. It can also be traced in the older suburbs, with their wide, straight streets and thin lines of trees. There are no twists and turns, no dips and curves in these suburban streets. You can see all there is to see up the street and down the street; and the houses, pleasant bungalows and villas peeping, as Caroline Carleton had said, from behind the shrubbery, have no dark places underneath and no attics either. It is rare to come across a house with a basement. There is simply nowhere for secrets, nowhere to hoard the personal past. There is nothing to conceal; almost, one might think, there is nothing to offer. Which doesn't mean there are no woodsheds, with whatever nastiness might be found there from time to time. But the past in Adelaide is a civic past; the personal is to be found in public places.

For a while then, the full impact of Colonel Light's plan of the city could be appreciated. The fact that it had an intelligent design had always been acknowledged, but what that meant for the experience of Adelaide had in some manner partly been lost from sight. Light had designed his city in much the manner of Philadelphia, a regular grid of streets forming a perfect square and surrounded by parklands. Perhaps there was intended a compatibility in the informing spirit of both Adelaide and Philadelphia, a like-mindedness of tolerance in religious and social governance. The design was however more perfect in summary than in application. One side of the notional square is a staggered set of steps and stairs, to provide defence against attack from the direction of the hills, we were told at school. More romance. It actually has something to do with a small creek wandering inconveniently across the parklands.

Within the city is a quincunx of town squares. The significant point is that there is nothing much at the centre of the city, except an endless argument about what to do with it – the city has moved up to one end, and has left a huge traffic island for Queen Victoria to survey, with an inappropriate fountain and a thin grove of deciduous trees to conceal the terminus of the Glenelg tramline, the sole remaining tramline, surviving because it had a dedicated track. The city has gathered by the river. Hallelujah brother.

The Adelaide plains are crossed by several natural watercourses called creeks, and one substantial creek called a river. This is dammed up behind a weir to form a reach of water just long enough for rowing eights to train on in the falling dusk. Occasionally, and for no apparent good reason, the gates of the weir are opened, the river is sluiced out, and the season's crop of stolen cash-registers can be retrieved from the foul sloppy mud. This whimsical practice is rather like pulling out the bath plug.

The River Torrens is, when it is not out, at the northern edge of the city. Most of what matters happens down by the Torrens – that is where the Cathedral and the Oval are, the Festival Hall, the old Parade Ground, Government House, the Museum and the Art Gallery, the University, the Botanic Gardens and the Zoo. More recently, the Casino. In South Australia you speak in these definite terms, as though there could be only one of everything. All the sounds of the city are channelled along it, but in that open space they take on a distant and purified quality, as in memory: the shunting and hooting from the old railway yards (these have now been relocated, and only a steadily diminishing local service remains), the *thwop thwop* from the Memorial Drive tennis courts, the chittering of revolving sprinklers and the far sharp cries of the piping shrike (peewee, Murray magpie, the state emblem), the peals of bells from St Peter's Cathedral. Time and space are held together here, not entranced but stabilised.

To take a walk along the riverbank, even though it is off to the edge of the city, is to find something of the special quality of Adelaide. Oh, do not ask 'What is it?' Let us go and make our visit.

The crushed gravel path begins somewhere up by the weir; perhaps it goes past the weir. On one side of the river it begins among poplar trees, on the other among bulrushes known as Pinky Flat. No doubt that was originally 'pinkeye': the occasional derro might be there in a stained navy suit or a greasy old overcoat, and hugging a wet paper-bag shaped like a flagon of sherry. It was once the territory of small boys and small dogs on their way to catch yabbies down below the weir, with a golf course over the way. There's a restaurant in there now, built in the heady days of throwing good money after bad, determined to change the character of the place, but in fact having to struggle with the inevitable reciprocity that persists in these matters.

Past the poplars, cautiously past the bend where the black swans have gathered on the grass to hassle sightseers both unwary and friendly; past the mounting stage for Popeye, a green and cream launch that takes families and tourists up and down the river so that they may see from the water exactly what they can see from the path; past the rotunda, a bandstand useful only as a vantage point at Carols by Candlelight, and where no band can be remembered as standing; past all these, the path leads to under the City Bridge, low enough and wide enough and gloomy enough with its concrete beams and arches, to form a kind of grotto. Now that the terrifying rumbling of the trams has disappeared, you can hear again the silence that encloses a hard echoing plink of water trickling from somewhere, and more distantly the klok of clumsy oarsmen in rowboats hired from Jolley's kiosk. From there, or as you walk further

along past the beds of zinnias towards the University foot-
bridge, you hear water-hens and ducks negotiating the rights
to the reeds, and students calling to each other at football
practice; and furthest away, beyond the end of the path where
all is stinkweed and litter, the sad aching moan of the lions
and tigers heaves over the rusting galvanised iron fence of
the Zoo, and drifts back down the river. Along the Torrens,
you are neither in nor out of the city, neither in nor out of
the daily round. You are however in a place which, as clearly
as any other I can think of, manifests the South Australian
sense of well-being. The senses are caught up and held
together here, and the on-going sameness of time is re-
affirmed. The quality of the light is unvarying, the openness
protected as in some very large sanctuary. It is a public place
with all the qualities of a private place.

Sunlight throws shadows, of course. There have been
some ugly episodes along the banks of the Torrens, and
strangers look nervously about them, suspicious of what
might lurk beneath or inside the tranquillity. Whatever
goes wrong in Adelaide happens just because of its openness, its innocence, its unsuspectingness. People do not
have the habit of living defensively, because it is not that
sort of place, or does not see itself as that sort of place.

North Terrace provides an alternative route. From
Government House, where just once at a Royal Levee society
matrons and the wives of aldermen forgot themselves, and
trampled down the agapanthus to get a better view – the
way I heard it, Royalty graced the grassy inner sanctum, the
more estimable and rapturous of Adelaide society percolated
about that in modest proximity; and the less worthy at
the outer perimeter, marked off by beds of the aforesaid
agapanthus, unable wholly to contain themselves, crashed
through the important markers of social cachet just as their

hairier sons and daughters when the Beatles came to town not too many years later. From there, following virtually right under the garden wall to the War Memorial, is another path through in effect a grove of plane trees and various others imported from the Old World. Throughout the summer they provide a light green canopy, a kind of shade and coolness that native trees don't attempt. Summer in Adelaide, however, is longer than the regulation three months; it lasts on and on through March and well into April. It would probably be more comfortable for all concerned to postpone the Festival of Arts by at least a month, but the time for that event has been set in concrete, as was the flower festival which preceded it. Each year, paying absolutely no heed to the facts of the South Australian climate, ladies from (one guesses) the better suburbs and from the more genteel associations, entered into a public competition of various displays of flowers. Large arrangements, stylish in the manner endorsed by Edwardian photographic studios, posed splendidly on the terraces outside Government House, in mute tribute to Vice-regality. On the lawns by the Anzac Memorial, viewing bridge provided, was the largest and most elaborate of the floral carpets, a maze of pansies and petunias and marigolds and whatever else would grow, every bloom as perfect as could be managed given the steadiness of the mercury at the top end of the scale for the last week or two. The Governor in his Vice-regalia would have awarded the prize yet again to the Country Women's Association, and the flowers proceeded to wither as sentimentally as could be expected. All that effort, for that fleeting moment in the early hours of judgement day. The Floral Festival died out, perhaps because the fashion for domestic English flowers died out, and South Australia's wildflowers are too rare, too understated for such extravagance. Yet the impulse to celebrate, to hold a festival, did not die out; it merely transformed itself. Not bread and circuses, but things of beauty and delight – a ritual of plenty and generosity when, given the thin brown land, its relative dryness and hardiness, one might have anticipated a more Spartan attitude. And after a sufficiently decent interval the wheel has turned again, and there is now a Rose Festival, reviving dreams of an earlier time and remembering the legendary display of Lady Barr Smith's driveway.

There it is again, that curious interplay which is not conflict, but another entrance into the South Australian ethos. Those women must have put extraordinary and sustained effort into the designing, the bringing to bloom of sufficient quantities of the needed flowers at just the same moment, at the most trying time of the year. To demonstrate what? They were invisible. I suppose in fact some of the ladies were hovering around somewhere; but once Lady Bonython had the whole thing going there was no individual kudos for all this extraordinary effort. And whatever one might have thought about the aesthetics of it, the masses of flowers all appearing there overnight not so much transformed that corner of Adelaide as confirmed its latent meaning.

What is revealed as true in Adelaide is true for the rest of the state. That combination of openness and stillness, of space and time, can be recognised when the almond blossom stands out against the foothills at Willunga. Make that the past tense, the developers found a higher calling in real estate. It is there magnificently along the vast length of the Aroona Valley in the northern Flinders Ranges, where the eye and the heart accept the softness that is within the apparent harshness of blue sky, red earth, violet haze of the Salvation Jane (not Paterson's Curse – those profane Easterners never could appreciate their blessings), the rustiness of the wild hops. Even the light white dust that spins above rubble outcrops of limestone has, at a distance, a lazy delicacy. Everywhere there is more to see, if only you look. It's an experience which isn't flaunted, isn't caught in holiday snaps. How do you photograph the marble air above the Coorong, so hot and dry you could not call it sea-spray? (You don't – you opt for the romantic transformation of 'Storm Boy' instead, splendid, powerful, Turneresque, but not what typifies the Coorong.) In that country without shade, where stumpy-tail lizards like sunbaked speckled turds are gasping on the hot bitumen, mirages shimmy all the way down the washboard roads and crows grate like old wind-mills, how can you tell about the smell and taste of dry stubble, or the powdery pink of a galah's feather, the softness of the bulrush heads? Or the thick dark stones in the creek bed, that make the sound of deep closed gorges when you throw them into a small pool. This is a country of much subtlety; but it does not declare itself openly. And how, other than converting it into another register, can you tell anyone else what it is like? It is a place of remarkable well-being, though not in the terms that others comprehend. *Ubicumque est bene ibi patria*, quoth Cicero.

That is why I do not accept the furtive, hugger-mugger gothicism of Barbara Hanrahan's Adelaide. She presumed romance again, to construct her fiction. It suited her imaginative interests to re-orientate the pattern of things to what happens in the sleep-out, on the path by the tank-stand (where *everyone* grew their ferns), in the back lanes – harmless territory but interesting because we were forbidden to go along them on our way home from school. Nothing happened down the lanes. Hanrahan writes *against* the experience of Adelaide, from various sources of anger, some personal no doubt and some, it seems, political and ideological and, or so it appears, acquired after the event. She railed against what she saw as the respectability and hypocrisy of the bourgeoisie. But that is a derivative notion imposed upon a place which is nothing like a nineteenth-century French township; and whatever its failings its complacency is of contentment, not smugness. External terms, somebody else's words – they are not a good fit, and in their distortion they presume the distortion inheres in the community. Hanrahan took up a romantic orientation, and that becomes the orientation of enclosure. It does not fit with the Adelaide which is really there, unassuming, standing back, basking in the good air.

The city all up one end, the Cathedral standing back to one side, tucked in between the Oval and the Women's and Children's Hospital, the place-sense which was concealed, revealed briefly and then lost again ... everything here is oblique, reticent. It is axiomatic that the essential things, the things of value, do not change. While in the panic of progress Adelaide may have lost sight of itself, it managed to evince its essential self in the characteristic manner of the people. By one of those coincidences so striking as to persuade you of its necessity, the character of the place and the dominant characteristics of dissent came together here. Paradoxically, in this manner which identifies the people, is to be found something which provides a firm correspondence with the national cultural mythology; for is this not also the basis of that old Australia-wide custom of bush etiquette, that simple courtesy which does not intrude or insist, which tells its stories indirectly, yet which quietly maintains its own integrity of vision – however comic or ironic the effect of that may be for the remote reader? For all we know, Adelaide, and South Australia, may be the most centrally Australian of the constituent communities.

2

A Piece of Fritz

If South Australians have a mostly well-preserved sense of modesty – we like to think this is one of our attributes, but we can hardly draw attention to it – it trips over itself in our readiness to point out that there were no convicts in our cultural background. I may already have remarked on this myself. We had no goldrush, and so no bushrangers, certainly none with their head in a bucket. No Eureka Stockade and no Lambing Flat riots, no blackbirding, no bomb attacks during the war. There is quite a lot South Australia does not have, including good water. No significant mountain range, no deep water harbour. Vast lakes with no water in them, a major river with no river-mouth. It becomes understandable why the habit of negative definition is so ingrained. It would never occur to us that there was anything enigmatic in affirming that 'there's no place like home'. We actually think we are defining what is, by affirming what is not.

Something else we are not doing is remembering the escaped convicts who joined with the sealers on Kangaroo Island or skulked about in the Adelaide Hills. And we are not remembering that the idea for planned settlement occurred to Edward Gibbon Wakefield while he was serving a prison sentence. Setting those unhelpful historical embarrassments to one side, part of the problem for South Australians is in having to meet others' assessments of what is significant, others' terms of measurement, others' valuations. In point of fact, we had our own; and the past tense is all. National marketing managers started straightening us out, re-arranging us to fit us into a national commodity – much like making sure we moved to the standard railway gauge, a more symbolic than practical amendment as train services began to be closed down anyway, and the only real trains were the ones that raced through the mid-north from Sydney to Perth, leaving Adelaide out on a branch-line.

We had, for example, our own understanding of what a loaf of bread was: two of what everyone else called loaves, joined face to face, and when torn apart exposing the choicest part of the loaf, which we called the baker's pinny. You could of course buy half loaves, and in the delicatessens you could even get a quarter loaf. We ordered double-cut rolls: they were cut right through, then each half sliced again, which meant you got twice the filling. We got these at the deli, as we called them, part milk-bar, part small-goods shop, part sandwich shop, not quite a corner-store. We called the little tubs of icecream we bought there 'dandies', in stubborn resistance to the rest of the country which seemed to have sold out to 'dixies', and incipient Americanism. I suppose there was some interstate take-over, and a national marketing manager determining it wasn't profitable to sell small servings of anything. And that the icecream-eating populace should become tubbier. Ah, where are the icecreams of yesteryear ... Industry started to become relocated in the eastern states, a process which was called centralising, and which meant that South Australia was being de-centralised. Other small businesses packed up and went west; some of them went bust, and some eventually became very successful as the Perth boom got under way. All this activity marked the end of the era I will be telling about, the fifties.

We had our own local names for what must have been nation-wide activities. When we gave someone a lift on our bike, we didn't dink or double dink, we donkeyed them. Freudians might have their own uncalled-for reflections on those pre-adolescent activities, but it is also tempting to find in that idiom a submerged awareness that the passenger was riding side-saddle, as on the iconic excursion to Egypt. Well, who is to say it was not so, in a generation which in very substantial proportion put in time at Sunday School? And of course we had our own way of saying, as well as our own words. To the uncouth ear, it may have seemed an affectation to hear 'vahz' and 'dahns' and so forth. Contrariwise, to us there was no warrant for the bandsaw horrors of the Sydneysiders' accent, and especially none for their wreckage of 'graph' and 'wrath'. And how Melburnians could pretend legitimacy for 'skerl' and 'perl' and 'cerl', and 'cassell' ... Pasties didn't taste right when they were pronounced with the short 'a'. As for 'paysties', that's what you might see in swinging Kings Cross.

The story was that pasties were developed by and for the Cornish miners who, by dint of their digging and delving, had arsenic on their hands, and so ate everything except the pastry ridge by which they held their lunch. As there had been scads of Cornish miners in the copper mines at Moonta and Kadina, we knew that not only pasties but also the way of pronouncing the word was ours. It wasn't as though we claimed any special prerogative for our own way of speaking; eastern sarcasm was a measure of their jealousy. We just knew that those who proposed themselves as our superiors and betters were a joke. It was obvious they were wrong. And pig-headed too, though it wasn't necessary to state the bleeding obvious. So we lived with the private comedy of eastern assumptions, as well as with the more potent and unfortunate tag-end of their presumptions.

Throughout these essays I am attempting to describe some of the cultural artefacts we did in fact have, and do still largely preserve; and to affirm, modestly of course, their value. Not that we always remarked on what was there. Why would we? It was what was familiar to us; in some sense, it was us. And so the habit of negative definition was re-inforced this way too. For example, and to return to where I began, the majority of us thought of ourselves as white, English ('Anglo-Saxon' is a later politically-attuned affectation) and Protestant. We didn't come across Catholics in the state schools, because they had corralled themselves in their own institutions, behind galvanised iron fences with the wallopers, the dreaded Christian Brothers. It didn't occur to us that some of the kids at primary school were part-Aboriginal. And so what if they were? They were just themselves: the Foleys, the Mundeys, the McNivens, and if they had any common characteristic it is that they were likely to be tough, they were good at running, they tended to live down towards the railway line. And some of them from time to time were disposed to not show up at school. That didn't seem at all surprising: nothing much happened in class so what was there to miss out on? Our education happened in slow motion; it didn't begin to speed up until secondary school, by which time their absence had became total. We were mainly a Protestant community because perhaps of the absence of convicts aforementioned – at least, that is how the history of the eastern states' experience seemed to stack up. Again, who knows? It is just the way it was, until the great waves of immigration, especially Italian, started to alter the imbalance. We were, in our own eyes, and by reputation, a homogeneous, stable and well-ordered community.

There was little self-consciousness within our community; or more precisely, within our generation. The preceding generation every now and then let drop its patronising attitude towards a largely invisible aboriginal presence. They were condescending to the ignorant speech patterns of those who said 'chimbley', who pronounced their 'haitches' and dropped their 'g's. We might have picked up on the implications, but it didn't stop us mirroring those regrettable vulgarisms when we kicked a footie in the street with the children of tramdrivers and meter-readers. And sometimes we got to experiment with a vocabulary we would never dare use at home. It was less risky to try it out on the children of teachers and ministers and doctors, who frequently surprised us with the lurid energy of their own vernacular. No doubt this awareness of differentiation could be read as a kind of discrimination. On the other hand, we were increasing our word power, and we were mastering the skills and strategies of diplomatic register. We joined the level of the group with whom we were speaking. We spoke with forked tongues.

We couldn't miss out on the very pointed suspicion of Catholics, who were known to be manoeuvring themselves into the public service, a deliberate strategy to grab power in the state (and, no doubt, with the effect of legitimating 'haitch'); but as we were not of an age to encounter the public service in its various manifestations, secular or denominational, that meant very little to us. We did not discriminate, we accepted whatever was the case. If a star winger in the district football team was known as 'Darkie', it didn't occur to us that that meant anything; it identified him, it was his name – just as the other players had nicknames: Macca, Killer,

Bluey. Bluey was a red-head, and the chances are that he was from a Catholic background, but who cared? Unless it meant he was naturally a left-kicker ... I understood the joke, but not why that was said of Catholics.

Slowly the ethnic and social mix of the school changed. The Jacomos brothers turned up from Greece and showed us how to play baseball. And their father ran a blue and white cafeteria and made the best hamburgers in Adelaide – there were always taxi-drivers taking their lunch break there – so they were bound to be popular. But they were likeable in their own right too. And Angie (Angelo) was the first kid I ever knew to wear his cap back-to-front. All that long ago. Children from various European countries arrived from time to time, from Poland and Yugoslavia and Byelorussia (where on earth was that?). Poms and Scots of course; inevitably. All fitted in, no more surprising or novel to us than the return of schoolmates who had been recovering from polio for a year or two.

The one group exceptional to all this inflow were the Italians, and it is puzzling to make this out. No doubt they went to Catholic schools, implying that the state schools weren't good enough for them. We had been told how cowardly the Italians were as soldiers, how ready to surrender (in subsequent reflection, this was probably very smart strategy), so maybe we were predisposed to contempt. One of the residues of war-time propaganda. Italian prisoners-of-war had been visible in the community in a way that no other group were, in their red and turquoise trousers. Many of them had worked quite happily on farms through the war, and the story was that they did not want to return to their homeland, they preferred to stay on here. Quite right too, but wasn't it for us to decide? If there were German or Japanese prison camps in South Australia in the forties, we didn't get to hear about it; their role as 'the enemy' had evaporated. It wasn't personal, somehow. Or maybe the propaganda hadn't been very effective, the Bluey and Curley comics notwithstanding. German equalled Jerry-built, not much good; made in Japan likewise invited suspicion about quality. In fact, the concept of 'the enemy' was curiously unreal. There was an invisible group of guerrillas in the Malayan jungles and there were large masses of troops in Korea, again all but invisible in face of the new war technology (and that absence of a visible antagonist underlies the whole sequence of *MASH*). In the Blackhawk comics, exemplary of the times, our heroes engaged with MIGs, not with whoever was flying them. We drew pictures of tanks and jet-fighters and spaceships all on the one page: technology carried our imagination into unrealised worlds, without human consequence. The kid sitting next to us at school was doing exactly the same, whatever past he (no mixed classes yet!) carried with him.

It didn't occur to us that we already had considerable variation in our cultural make-up; that we had always had a remarkable degree of – how does one put it? – natural assimilation. Our history was full of it. Colonel William Light, the man with the vision of what Adelaide might become, was born in Penang, which his father founded, and of a Eurasian mother rumoured, fancifully, to be a Malayan princess. Whatever the connection between his parents, it was both irregular and exotic; yet not extraordinary enough to contribute to a conviction. In the legal sense, not that of belief. Not everyone was mutton-chop whiskers and Methodist, as in the popular if unfounded (a choice adjective in this instance) impression.

With the incursion of great groups of migrants in the forties and fifties came visible changes in the community at large. A few sandwich shops started tentatively to re-jig themselves as coffee lounges. Restaurants stayed open for evening meals and gradually wine began to appear on the tables. Against terrible odds, there was an attempt to keep some kind of activity in the city after the shops had shut. We were undergoing a culture change. And there was very quickly a major soccer league: the years of struggle by English and Scottish immigrants to get Australian laddies to take up the real football ('aerial ping-pong', our uncles scoffed) was overwhelmed by a new competition based on national groups: Juventus, Orange, Austria, Beograd, Croatia, Olympic ... It should have been a good idea. Certainly the local ethnic groups got behind their teams, and affirmed their own national loyalties. But antagonisms which had come with them from Europe also surfaced, and rivalries were not just about the teams' performance on the field. The crowds not only barracked for their teams, but against the opponents' supporters. Adelaide hadn't seen anything like this kind of passion, this kind of intensity, unless at the infamous Bodyline Test, and it didn't like it. This was no longer sport; this was uncomfortable. It was unAustralian, as then understood. It was incipient multiculturalism, the assertion and maintenance of ethnic identities, in team sports and social clubs and restaurants, and although we didn't know it, it was going to change our way of life.

Our elected representatives, transforming themselves as they do into our betters, were complicit in this social re-engineering. The South Australian Housing Trust evolved a whole new city, to be named Elizabeth by and for the visiting Queen. It was out on the hot northern plains, the houses were all pretty much of the same size and alignment, and the native shrubs took some time to establish themselves. The new residents, almost wholly from England and

Scotland, likewise. No doubt it was better than a migrant camp, but it was completely without interest. It was somewhere to drive past, at a distance, on the way to such other engaging attractions as the racing circuit at Mallala, or the Hummocks at the top of the Gulf. It took time to set up sufficient industry in the new city for adequate employment; it quickly developed a reputation for grievance, for troublemaking of one kind or another. I don't know what exactly we had expected – perhaps that in developing this satellite city the government had set up the basis for another version of ourselves. Assuming, of course, that those who came to settle among us would want to merge with us, become like us. Who wouldn't? And if they whinged, then they were ungrateful and could go right back where they had come from, and good riddance. We were on the cusp of the great decade of consciousness-raising, of being made self-conscious; and as a corollary, of identifying and acknowledging the invisible other. We were about to be different; whether that is altogether an improvement, who can say? It is just the way things turned out, and we were subsequently required to cope with it as best we could.

Curiously, none of this was new. Wakefield's English experiment had been doctored from the start. Within just a couple of years of first settlement, indeed almost within a matter of months, groups of Germans, Lutheran dissenters mainly, some refugees from resurgent Catholic aggression, were arriving in South Australia, off-loading in small boats at Port Misery, as old Port Adelaide was initially and understandably known. The ships could not get close in to the harbour, such as it was; they had to stand out to sea to avoid the sandshoals. The passengers were rowed in as far as they could come, and then sailors carried them the rest of the way in through the shallows. I am not aware that this courtesy was extended to livestock; it might well explain why South Australian sailors got as far away as the deep water harbours of Nova Scotia.

Whole groups migrated, under the leadership of a pastor, who seemed to have much the authority of a rabbi – the comparison suggests itself. There are stories of engaged young women being asked to break off their engagement and instead to marry a man whose wife had died on the voyage, and whose young children were in need of a mother. The survival of the new generation was paramount, and personal wishes were set aside for the greater good. This was a strongly-disciplined religious group, and they proved hard-working and highly principled when they settled at Klemzig out on the Adelaide plains, and Hahndorf up in the Hills. But as they had almost no English, they were not readily employable. The Klemzig group quickly became the providores of fresh vegetables to Adelaide; the Hahndorf group formed a different and increasingly separate enclave. The same division happened when the next groups settled in the Barossa Valley, and later again in the Murray mallee, the scrublands along the Murray.

The Germans contributed variously to the cultural make-up of early South Australia, vigorously re-inforcing the strong grain of independence that went along with religious convictions of dissent. Catherine Helen Spence in the early novel *Clara Morison* remarked not only on the industriousness of the German settlers, but on the distinctiveness of their cottages – they were defining their own architectural features. 'Annie would point out a short-waisted, broad-paling house, of which the bright red door and windows marked it as in-contestably a German edifice.' Other German families made a more spectacular statement: there is still to be seen a hollow gum tree in which one family lived, I think the Herbigs.

They were tough; they were also probably destitute. They survived. The gum tree too, apparently. These were not people given to ornamentation: that was a function of both the lack of economic resource and of their strict religious upbringing. Their houses were plain, and so were their churches and halls, though the severity had a certain charm, as the Hahndorf Academy, the first German language school and now the Hans Heysen gallery, displays. There is little wasteful detail: limited roof overhang, minimal porches, small windows and narrow verandahs.

Not all of them went on the land; some were professional people. The German farmers acquired a reputation for scratching a living where others could not. As they could not afford prime pasturage they took up what acreage they could get, in scrubby country much of it – and made a future for themselves by dint of sheer hard work, battling against the odds, and contrary to local practice, with mixed farming. In something like a model for the Dad and Dave stories, the entire family contributed to the running of the farm. In time the family home would become established, and perhaps the eldest son would marry and be given a modest place on the property. As the family fortunes improved the second son married and a slightly better place could be provided, and so on down through the siblings; with the inevitable result that the youngest was left with the family home. It wasn't a pattern that the British settlers understood, or wanted to imitate. But on the struggling family farms in the German settlements it was accepted, and had its own irrefutable logic in such an economy; and it was another expression of that early stern discipline.

As I have been suggesting, this wasn't a single community at all, in the narrow sense, though the immediate effect of their sturdy self-reliance amounted to a kind of segregation.

Yet before long the German contribution flowed over into the mainstream. Lutherans and Methodists sometimes shared the same church, turn and turn about, in the smaller country towns; George Fife Angas, a prominent Methodist, had been the early sponsor of German immigration. German cooking began to percolate into the Anglo cuisine, and vice versa as it could be said they shared a common determination to make sure the lamb roast was sizzled to pieces. The one area of self-gratification they permitted themselves was in indulging their sweet tooth. Home cooking was full of butter, cream, jam, currants and sultanas. If the main course was immense in point of quantity, the deserts were overwhelming in point of variety. German cakeshops served up strudel, streusel, cream cakes – though it might be argued that Queen Victoria's German husband had given his particular blessing to those. One particular bun, a yeast bun with a jam and artificial cream filling, we knew as a Kitchener bun – but it had started out in life as a Berlin bun.

That name change came at about the same time as a number of comparable attempted cancellations of the German presence in the South Australian community, initiated by a report to the South Australian parliament in 1916 and implemented in the following year ('the names of all towns and districts in South Australia which indicate a foreign enemy origin should be altered, and ... such places should be designated by names either of British origin or South Australian native origin'). German-language schools were closed down. Towns were re-named. Hahndorf became Ambleside. The railway station continues to be known by its pretty new English name, but the village stubbornly returned to its true identity in the mid-thirties. Klemzig, where the market gardeners had started business, was re-designated Gaza, to commemorate the recent activities of the AIF. That was not a name which caught on either. The attempt to replace Lobethal with Tweedvale never stood a chance. Germantown Hill was successfully re-incarnated as Vimy Ridge, but the original name was re-applied nearby to the long pull up the eastern slope of the hills. A few other such transpositions prevailed, given the unassailable provenance of the new title: Birdwood for Blumberg, Verdun for Grunthal. It is an interesting reflection of the times that when Aboriginal words were used as substitutes for the German place-names, they tended to prevail, e.g. Marree instead of Herrgott Springs. A good thing too: it would be just too confusing to think of the Afghan cameldrivers' retirement home at an oasis dedicated to Herr Gott, when and where thanks might more properly be accorded to Allah. Marree says it like it is. One curiosity is that the Hundred (i.e. district) of Rhine South was re-named the Hundred of Jutland. Go figure, as the young now say.

One place name which did not attract this patriotic renovation was Adelaide itself, named after the German wife of King William: Adelheid Amalie Luise Theresa Carolin of Saxe-Meiningen. She had of course already anglicised her own name, but it is a nice instance of the compatibility of the two groups and the artificiality of the exclusion. And another instance of what the citizens do not remember because they do not register the distinction.

We had German names all around us. Everywhere were Henschkes and Heuzenroeders and Heckendorfs, Lehmanns and Lindners and Lindrums, Paechs and Rohdes, Schroeders and Schwerdts, Thieles and Tozers, Vogelsangs, Weidenhoffers and Wundtkes. They were shopkeepers and piano-teachers, sportsmen and schoolmasters, doctors and housepainters and policemen; and farmers, farmers, farmers, some of whom, experts in dry-land farming, established themselves on new properties on the western plains in New South Wales, or Queensland. The descendants of the German settlers were just like everyone else – though maybe there was a percentage of straight fair hair. Or a percentage of very thin hair; the wingnut look was not unknown among them. They were third and fourth and even fifth genera-tion South Australians, and their pioneering forefathers had readily sworn allegiance to Queen and country. Their endeavour had been to fit in, and until the tourism agencies got revved up, lederhosen were not seen in the Barossa or elsewhere. But the Tanunda brass band had pumped away across all the years, and liedertafel had been maintained to some extent across the intervening generations. The local histories say so did the skittle alleys, Kugelbahn, but if so that wasn't anything the rest of us knew about. Wendt the jeweller was for many years one of the highly reputable businesses in Adelaide. The Menz biscuit company got bought out and their distinctive biscuits immediately disap-peared from the supermarket shelves. Another blessing from the taste-challenged commissars of commerce. Seppelt the winemaker built an ostentatious winery in the Barossa, and overcame attempted re-naming of the area as Dorrien. That was never going to work. Lindrum was a billiard-table man-ufacturer and billiard-player. And the man who wrote the music for Caroline Carlton's 'Song of Australia' was Carl Linger.

It may seem curious that wine-making, and especially German-family wine-making, took so long to become widely appreciated. To begin with, wine was for winos, a sorrier version of the deros who carried bottles of McWilliams' sherry in their overcoat pockets. Nobody drank wine: it was all either beer or spirits. And yet it was there to be discovered, especially Leo Buring's riesling. The long road to temperance perdition invariably began with hock and lemon, a drink acceptable to the daughters of the establishment. In the late fifties or thereabouts the masses began to find their unhappy way to Porphyry Pearl and Sparkling Starwine; and Kaiser Stuhl meant without exception sparkling rosé, promoted I seem to recall at the first Festival of Arts. It seems we liked our wines sweet at that time; German-style. Arguably, they were much less damaging than the rough reds. Later generations have been very sensible in re-dressing their forefathers' oversight. Besides, the drinking water has become appreciably (is that the word?) worse.

Chief of all, we had fritz. Whenever we went to the butcher's, we would be given a piece of a fritz. It didn't occur to us to think of this as German sausage. It was fritz. Devon, only better. It came sheathed in a distinctive orange skin, the colour of a Penguin paperback; and it was probably a bit more than two inches in diameter, so that the butchers were being quite generous in their hand-outs. Fritz was what you put in your sandwiches, along with Rosella tomato sauce – between two slices of Golden Crust Bakery white bread spread with South Australian Farmers' Union butter. 'Fritz', it turns out, was the popular name of Johann Eisenberg, who emigrated to Lobethal in 1883 and soon set up a stall in the East End market, specialising in German meats. And Fritz's German sausage became known far and wide as fritz, or so it is claimed. More important for the custom that still prevailed when I was able to benefit from it, he used to give children a piece of sausage while their parents decided on what to purchase. And that largesse has continued in the stalls at the Central Market.

Fritz Eisenberg was interned during World War I, as were many others. Farmhouses were searched for guns: some families had to hide such verboten heirlooms as muskets from the Battle of Waterloo for example – those would have been from Blucher's troops, not Wellington's. So much for the glorious alliance, and so much for history, the history we didn't have and didn't want to know about. By the Second World War, German ancestry was no longer an issue. Either the community had become more tolerant, or the descendants of Germans had made a concerted and successful effort to become indistinguishable from Anglo-Australians. It is interesting that with the new soccer league there was not a German team. The young men had become outstanding cricketers and football players – Australian Rules, that is.

The German community had certainly become respectable. Hans Heysen had inherited the role of leading landscape painter from the Heidelberg School (another pertinent place-name) and began interpreting the South Australian landscape, especially of the Flinders Ranges, in softened tones and sentimental arrangements – the pastoral beatitudes of Streeton transposed. I knew a woman who had cooked for him when he was painting along the Murray, herself from a local German family, and with heaps of traditional recipes up her rolled sleeves. She was a solid chunky woman, with a face dark and gnarled as a lump of mallee. She was not unlike Catherine Helen Spence's description of German cottages in early colonial Adelaide: short-waisted and broad paling-ed ... She was not at all interested in his paintings, but she could recall what he liked to eat. Eating was a serious business. For her and, apparently, for Heysen. Ted Strehlow relocated to Adelaide from the Hermannsburg Mission, where Albert Namatjira had commenced another kind of landscape interpretation. Robert Helpmann is an inversion of all this, confrontational as ever in doubling the final consonant of his name, when he first arrived in London in the mid-thirties. To his mind it was impressive to appear 'foreign'. His family were in fact respectably Anglo, property owners for several generations.

None of all this German colour was particularly notice-able. German was not heard on the streets or in the play-grounds, probably because of the closure of German language schools towards the end of the First World War. After the Second World War a number of linguistic anthropologists arrived from Germany, fascinated to discover that where some of the elders still spoke the language of their forebears, they spoke it as a residual late eighteenth-century or early nineteenth-century language. It had not adjusted to its new circumstances but had survived, more or less intact. But with fewer and fewer of the locals able to use it. Whether or how much the presence of the German-speaking community contributed to mainstream English in the state is still pretty much a blank. We were aware of words like 'shemozzle' just as other Australians were; whether we were any more predis-posed to use such expressions than the national average, ulti-mately Yiddish terms many of them, is for experts to assess. It is possible they gave us 'mullygrub', i.e. mallee grub, a kind of indefinite term for a younger person but meaning some-thing like 'scallywag'. My grandfather's equivalent was 'mug-wump', which he explained as a bird sitting on a fence with its mug on one side and its wump on the other. He once stood for parliament, and no doubt had a range of private political jokes we never did catch on to. If there were German incursions into local English usage, it had become so thor-oughly integrated as to be indistinguishable. Young men of German extraction served in the AIF in the Second World War, the premier refused to close down the surviving German-language schools (as the RSL had urged), and the leaders of the Lutheran Church re-affirmed their loyalty to Australia and the Empire. German South Australians had not only merged with the dominant British stock; they *were* us.

Much the same had happened among the Cornish

community associated with the copper mines at Moonta and Kadina, and before that at Burra, in their time the richest copper mines in the British Empire. The Cousin Jacks, they were called, and in Oswald Pryor's amusingly dour cartoons they are all elderly, bearded, waist-coated and tenacious of their own limited view of things. 'Near 'nough b'aint good enough, got to be 'zact.' ''Tis 'zact.' 'That be near enough then.' The great days of the Moonta male choir were well and truly over, the huge Methodist church there no longer filled to capacity, and we failed to connect the Treglowns and Tretheweys and Tregenzas with this part of our past. Cornishness was pretty much encapsulated in our Uncle Tom's senile pet galah which, he told us, couldn't speak Cornish but could whistle it. Cornishness was confined to the pasties and the cartoons, depictions of figures that had grown old, and not knowing that this was no longer their prime. So with the German component in South Australia: if you thought of them as in any sense a separate group, the figures that came to mind were the old-timers, unyielding in the face of change, wary of the expression of success. To an extent, superstitious about that. Case-hardened and stalwart.

There was a comic book in circulation then or there-abouts, 'The Katzenjammer Kids'. It was in fact an American comic, but not so as you'd notice. It was our sole window into German-ness as something distinctive from our own range of experience, and the comic point was that the elders, Mama, der Captain who boarded with them, and the long-coated, long-bearded Inspector, were inflexible caricatures, pompous and over-bearing. The Katzenjammer twins were adventurous, always breaking across the proscribed bound-aries. They were I suppose progressives within a conservative regime. They were just like any other kids. They were prob-ably brats. They invariably got into trouble, and the cartoon strip would end with them being turned over and spanked on der Captain's knee, or on the table or some other convenient piece of furniture; and Rollo the goodygoody cousin, always an observer at a cautious distance, would comment with smug satisfaction that they had brought it upon themselves. If young Australians were by national definition Ginger Meggs, these were our cousins-german, looking for a degree of independence but more constrained by the family enclave, especially by the authority vested in the father figure. And as with 'Ginger Meggs', so with 'The Katzenjammer Kids', the depiction was of a life and times that was receding into the past, yet still recognisable to us.

What do you do with this pumpernickel profusion? With this cultural diversity? Nowadays, it is exploited. Oktoberfest, Schützenfest, back to Moonta days, street parades, ethnic dancing: that is, costume-culturalism. It is a part of the modern political agenda. In the fifties, you did nothing at all about it. We certainly did not celebrate it. It was the given condition, our cultural background, all blended and witching in harmony as Caroline Carlton and Carl Linger had exulted in their anthem. Blending did not mean surrendering. But it did mean that ethnicity was a largely invisible factor, uncontroversial (the RSL notwithstanding), a shimmer and gleam in the spectrum that made up the cultural mix. It was not a marker of differentiation, and did not become so until at some stage in the sixties when we were taught to acknowledge the priority of otherness, important as that undoubtedly is, over communal cohesion. 'United in the common good', as the state's motto proclaims. The achievement of the German community is to have demonstrated so successfully how that is put into practice. They defined us, more than themselves.

3

The Custom of That Country

Imagine this. A summer evening in one of the city parks; any city will do. Velvety sky, a slight breeze off the harbour, the river, the hills, whichever, and no dew. You are listening to the Symphony Orchestra under the stars; you are sitting well back in the crowd. Someone with a big smile but a dreadful nasal intonation is massacring 'Carnival of the Animals'. The amplifiers are echoing badly, the orchestra at that distance sounds plastic and looks dislocated.

It is the immediate spectacle that overwhelms – the snogging couples, people endlessly stepping over and occasionally on each other, or stumbling over empty bottles, kids bored and aggrieved, the smell of ravaged chicken carcasses, the long queues at the banks of portaloos. Can you imagine that?

These are not the too fastidious objections of one with reverential assumptions about what is due to Symphony under the Stars, or Opera in the Park, or the ballet, or even Carols by Candlelight; nor a mental genuflection before the arts-that-really-matter. Rather, they register a dismay at the lack of the sense of occasion itself. Boorish behaviour was undoubtedly just as prominent and just as objectionable at the Colliseum or at the Globe, so it ought not to be a surprise when it is found sprawling on blankets under the figtrees, indifferent to what is going on. It is a specific example of what D.H. Lawrence identified, in *Kangaroo*, as inherent in the levelling tendency of Australian hedonism. He may not have had in mind the horizontal writhing of the modern era; he was, after all, a bit of a prude when push came to shove.

Watching the stars – and no, not those pastry-faced frauds strutting their tedious hour upon the stage, rather the ones that twinkle in the broad reach of the heavens – one has more sense of connection with the vast continuum than with one's impertinent neighbour rolling on to the edge of your blanket.

And that sense of natural and perhaps even spiritual connection, those occasionally perceived pledges of continuity, are of enormous importance in a country such as this, with its largely (or is it narrowly?) indifferent attitude to setting down cultural roots, sporadic as these are. 'A society requires antecedents,' George Steiner wrote in *In Bluebeard's Castle*. 'Where these are not naturally at hand, where a community is new or reassembled ... a necessary past tense to the grammar of being is created by intellectual and emotional fiat.' Our customs identify the very character of our culture, and we can ill afford casually to dispense with either. Whatever intrinsic meaning any surviving custom has, and whatever individual meaning any custom has for each of us, it also has a social value by virtue of being a custom. One property of custom is that it allows each of us to find his, or as we add these days, denying cadence but affirming gender, her relation to it.

These notions are fostered by the approach of Christmas. The marketing managers ensure it. They have their own tribal rituals, as fixed and as obviously self-interested as the annual brewery strikes used to be at the lead-up to Christmas. Each year we are told through television and the press that this is not going to be a happy Christmas for retailers, that the stores are not doing well. And then the annual Christmas miracle: there are record-breaking sales in the last days before Christmas. Every year. It's enough to reinstate your faith in providence, or in commerce, whichever seems to matter the more to you. And just as re-assuring as the staged and managed crises in real estate. The modern world has organised meaningful new patterns for itself, and ambiguously thanks us for our custom.

Whatever precise religious significance Christmas has for each of us, it is also a season of celebration, of festival; a season of quaint customs based in obscure ritual, and now potent in their secular manifestation, whatever their archetypal basis (such as the winter games that displace the calamity of the death of the year). Christmas comes but once a year, an old rhyme tells us; it is, to repeat the point, a season of approach, of the about-to-be, of imminence as well as immanence. As those customs all reach back into the past, so the past is gathered up into the present. And that is enriching, at least to those who observe those customs. On the other hand, the commercial hype of Christmas is to enrich the shareholders, and everyone is happy.

We tend to downgrade the present in these matters. We are convinced Christmas isn't what it used to be. We can prove that by going into any department store, where the bells of the cash registers ding dong merrily on hire purchases, and muzak, not choirs of angels, does the honours in exultation. Whatever happened to the magic of Christmas, one may ask. Perhaps it never was magical. That was a sentimental notion peddled by Christmas card manufacturers and Hollywood, Scrooge's humbug. Or perhaps it is becoming another victim of our communal disposition to subvert our own values, by wilfully ignoring the efficacy of custom.

For one thing, the proportions have changed. More and more we are pressed to participate collectively. Just as we are corralled into consensus politics, so we are shepherded into all sorts of social activities, including the celebrations of the season. Christmas was once very much a family matter, a fairly domestic set of ceremonies, though shared by just about the entire community. Nowadays it is marked as a kind of mass entertainment – Carols by Candlelight, for example, which didn't arrive as I recall until the mid-fifties, that is, at much the same time as television, and where either there is nothing to do but watch a procession of passé showbiz and television personalities (there's a contradiction in terms for you) do their nasty solitary act in front of the crowd, or the lax masses are jollied on to make a good show for the TV viewers. Certainly the singing of carols is about singing together, but that just doesn't happen with either joy or spontaneity on the banks of the Yarra or the Torrens. Everything has to be organised; this has become yet another programmed concert. Whereas what I recall about Christmas past is, above all else, that it used to happen inside the family; and maybe that is still the best part of our Christmas customs.

My earliest memories of Christmas have to do with Christmas Eve. No, none of that commonplace cuteness about stockings and visions of sugar plums. On Christmas Eve we went to my grandparents' dark brown house, my father's parents'. It was a house full of curtains and heavy cedar furniture. Aunts and uncles and various degrees of cousins, never sighted at other times, were all there – and so was the tree, in the front room. But nobody was allowed in yet. There were games to be played outside in the dark – kneeling at a bowl full of water and apples, near where the collie was fed. That was also where the path went down to the outside lav, with its big fluted yellow bowl, stained like a cigarette smoker's teeth. You could spend a long time looking in that bowl, a kind of funnel into mermaid country you thought, perhaps because of the elaborate ornamentation on the porcelain; but you would be told to hurry up because there were lots of agitated cousins-at-a-remove who had had too much raspberry cordial to drink.

Organised games were played at the back of the house while, I realised later, presents were wrapped and labelled and put under the Christmas tree. Then we were let inside to supper, and then down the hall, like a tunnel in time, to the front room; and here Christmas really happened. My mother played the piano and we all sang carols and the sorts of songs everyone sang then, that is the sorts of song the generation before that used to sing, 'Little Brown Jug' and 'D'ye Ken John Peel'; and they seemed apt enough for Christmas. We might even have a squashed up session of doing the hokey pokey, which wasn't about Christmas but about getting us to let off a bit of steam. And then she might play a bit of Chopin, or 'The Rustle of Spring', while we stared hard at the mound of wrapped shapes under the tree, and tried to work out which might be ours. And no one could make a move as we were all crowded in, adults on chairs and arms of chairs, children on laps or at the knees of parents, all drawn back because – with a jolly rousing version of 'Jingle Bells' – Father Christmas came clumping down the long dark passage and burst into the room, ringing a brass bell and dancing like a crazed thing around and around in the centre of us all; danced, indeed, like Dad Rudd with a bull-ant up his trouser leg, all knees and beard and elbows. It was as good as a pantomime.

It was Grandma of course, my older brothers would tell me. It was and it wasn't. She had on my uncle's flying boots, the boots he had worn as a rear-gunner based in Darwin – he had only seen one Japanese aircraft through the entire war, so it wasn't much of a war either for him or for us. We reckoned the mark in the fur lining (fur lining in Darwin!) was a blood-stain; and that he had probably shot himself in the foot to get it, so as to impress. And she had a pillow up her front, and too much red on her cheeks and nose, and a straggly beard like a goat's armpit. Dancing like that, she wasn't quite Grandma either; but in any case you forgot your scepticism when she sat down next to mother on the piano seat and gathered her puff and started doling out the presents, some from a sugar bag as well as the other strange-shaped ones under the tree. Father Christmas seemed to know a bit too much about what each of us had been up to through the year, so that we had an uneasy time of it before the presents came our way.

After all the unwrapping and showing and comparing, it was 'Jingle Bells' again and more antic leaping and hopping around the room and up the passage and out the front door – you could hear it slam – and then time to tidy up and remember your manners and thank everyone and you were tired because it was so late and still a long drive home. And there was Grandma again, saying goodnight at the front door and telling us how, if we kept watching the moon, we'd see Father Christmas's sleigh going across the sky; and I saw it, I really did, and I don't care how my brothers scoffed.

Some years we were taken in to one of the big department stores in the city, John Martin's, to visit the Magic Cave. The least important part of that was the studio Father Christmas. We knew intuitively that he wasn't the one that mattered, and besides it was always embarrassing to have to sit on his lap, or stand inside his knees, and worse still to have to invent an answer to the big question. Because you didn't really want anything for Christmas. You just wanted Christmas.

The Magic Cave was fascinating, but it wasn't about

magic, in spite of the fairy helper. There was a huge rocking horse called Nipper: it trembled as its rockers crushed the ridges in the floorboards, and its great wooden teeth came gnashing down on the children standing in line, waiting their turn for a ride. Nipper was for some reason the high point of the Christmas pageant too. He had a companion, another giant horse called Nimble, but Nipper was the favourite by a long nose. Near to that, in a kind of cage, an endless column of toy soldiers – not the colourful Nutcracker Suite kind, but all in jungle fatigues or tommy helmets – and tanks and fieldguns rattled across a war zone and disappeared over a ridge, teasingly ambivalent about whether the war was really over.

Family patterns change. Soon Christmas was held at our other grandparents', a big house white and bright and down by the beach. Here everything happened out in the open. They had a young-ish Norfolk Island pine growing in the back garden, which served as both Christmas tree and canopy. Over the years my grandfather had kept on topping the crown out of it, so that it ended up sadly compressed, an enormous tasselled beach umbrella. When we sat, we sat in its shade; we were sitting under the Christmas tree.

When we didn't sit, we were racing about on the beach, throwing sea sponges. At moments of adult inattentiveness we would be allowed to scramble up a series of metal rungs ripening and rusting in the salt air, up to a flat deck behind the parapet at the front of the house. It was rather like the cubic plywood models of the houses in Bethlehem that we were shown at Sunday School. From there, high above the esplanade, we looked out to see what ships were sailing by.

Or while my grandfather held court among the aunts, we played cricket in the driveway with the uncles. They would suggest gravely to each other that one or other of the young fellers showed a bit of promise, or bowled a good line, and would make his mark one of these days; and we would get hotly pleased with ourselves, make a rash shot and do in our chances for future selection for the district teams; or too enthusiastic, hit the balding tennis ball over the wall for six. The uncles would wink, and sidle off somewhere for a cigarette and a bit of a talk, until ferreted out again by all the imploring nephews.

When the day began to grow cool, or the uncles declared because of bad light and the need of a cup of tea, when the aunts had finished the clatter and clack of their washing up, we all trooped inside for a general exchanging of presents. My mother would wipe her hands and play the piano – perhaps 'The Rustle of Spring' – and then there would be a few carols and a general decision to head off before it got too dark, because it was a fair drive home, a good league hence, and the children were all tired. These were marvellous afternoons that stretched on and on, unvarying in their unfolding simple pattern, and you fitted contentedly right inside them.

Yet there was change too, even as the repetition confirmed itself. Gradually we became aware of a wider social context of Christmas, but also of a narrower one. Christmas became more firmly centred on the immediate family. The season began with the first 'Father Christmases', thistle-seeds like a star-burst of cat-whiskers that drifted in with the hot summer breezes from the northern plains, or perhaps from building allotments throughout the expanding suburbs. If you caught one of them, you held it in your cupped hands, whispered to it what you wanted for Christmas, and blew it away. Father Christmases caught in cobwebs or under cupboards didn't count.

But as that wasn't of much assistance to our parents, we

were encouraged to write out a list of what we wanted, and if ever we saw a blackbird sitting on the chimney pot we had to rush inside and throw our list up the chimney vent. The blackbird was supposed to swoop down and carry it off to who knows where. As in the excitement of doing all this before the bird flew away we always forgot to put our address on the letter, we couldn't complain if Father Christmas didn't deliver the goods as per request.

At school we began to make our own Christmas cards. All through primary school the same design: two sprigs of holly, like batwings, in one corner of the card, two bells in another corner tolling? pealing? anyway, forever unheard, the clapper sticking out like a rude tongue, and inside the message that got muddled each year: *Happy Christmas and a Merry New Year*.

As Christmas got nearer, the apricots began to ripen on the trees. In every backyard were apricots, plums, peaches, nectarines, various kinds of grapes. Neighbours would trade satsumas for blackcurrants or muscatels, and as though there weren't enough cooking to do for Christmas, there were now preserves to be bottled, jam to make and fruit to stew in the big aluminium pan you had borrowed to make your blasted ginger beer – so-called for its violent explosive properties. The whole house was a rich fume of fruit cakes, fruit slices, fruit puddings. Every now and then, when we had all caught up with ourselves, there might be a quiet family evening. If we weren't cracking almonds for pocket money, we might play ludo or dominoes or, later, monopoly, or make rude shadows on the wall; and mother would practise a few carols on the piano, or perhaps 'The Rustle of Spring'. That always made her feel good, as good as having a cup of tea, she said. And then it would be time to put up the decorations, always in pretty much the same place, and the room would smell of the dry crinkling of crepe paper, and teeth-tingling tinsel; and because it was hot we would sit out in the kitchen, the coolest room in the house, and drink glasses of fruit punch with cold tea in it, or if it had turned out to be a good batch, some of the home-made ginger beer. In the still of the evening perhaps you could hear truck loads of young people singing carols several streets away; and on a Friday night the distant roar of the speedway. Those nights before Christmas were characteristically still and bright, just like in the carols; it was no surprise at all to think of the midnight as clear, for it always was, except once when a wisp of cloud, was it, had crossed the moon.

At last it would be Christmas morning. There was always something in the pillow-cases hung on the end of the bed – blue rubber daggers and clock-work motorbikes and a Tiger Tim annual, a kazoo, a packet of Japanese paper flowers that unfolded and expanded mysteriously and beautifully in a glass of water, a tin box of paints or a double-decker wooden pencil-case. While no doubt like any small boy I was simply unappreciative of what Father Christmas had bought – never Santa, that crass commercial Nick-come-lately – the stronger recollection is instead of the family drifting in to the front room, gathering around the Christmas tree, to open presents and eat breakfast and create a huge litter all over the floor, the only day in the year that that would be tolerated, even I imagine encouraged. It was all done in a leisurely, comfortable way; there was no tearing frenzy, no piranha-like ravaging of the pile of presents that had suddenly accumulated under the tree on the previous evening. So we sat about for the best part of the morning, fiddling with the things we had got, flipping through books, eating fingers of toast, drinking cups of tea.

Until suddenly, my stars! Look at the time. The morning

had become the afternoon, and there would be a mad scramble to get the Christmas dinner ready. The afternoon was just entering its hottest phase; the blinds were closed to shut out the heat, and we all sat down to eat our way through the biggest meal of the year. An endless procession of sourgrapes nationalists, wowsers of custom, have denounced this practice as an absurdity. But custom is not about commonsense, it runs by its own conventions. Besides, who, having eaten roast lamb for fifty-one weekends in a row, would pass up the chance for chicken or duck or turkey? This was a table to look forward to, to sit down to, to enjoy.

Most years my father tried to take a photograph of – well, it still isn't clear just what he thought he could photograph, though one understands his impulse. Here was his family, all brought together at one table; the symbolism was apt, the sentiment a domestic version of the sense of community. But you couldn't photograph it. Besides, he was never master of the camera. Something always went wrong, and year after year the dinner went cold while he tried to get the flash to work, or the automatic timer, or he went to see if he had a new film. He forgot to take off the lens cap, or he didn't notice that some balloons were in the way; and the more we protested or chiacked, the more he would get cross. 'Happy Christmas' someone would suggest *sotto voce*, but then there would be the pulling of crackers and blowing whistles and reading out jokes made as well as printed in Taiwan or somewhere with an equally inscrutable sense of humour, and the potential storm cloud had vanished into an accelerating jollity. By the time of the Christmas pudding, with its charms and threepences and sixpences (inevitably whoever got the bachelor button would get the miniature porcelain baby), genial disorder ruled: paper hats had sagged or torn or discoloured, wisecracks and comments flew here and about, always intercepted and knocked askew from one side, and pity help any occasional guest trying to make sense of it. Yet sense there was, the inclusiveness of close kinship asserting itself.

My mother determined to develop a family tradition, an addition to but no essential part of custom; each Christmas she would bring to the table some new and exotic food – perhaps reindeer tongue one year, or whale meat or frog-legs or witchetty grubs or whatever unlikely rather than bizarre provender she could find. This was usually more acceptable as an idea than in fact. I remember the year of the chocolate-coated ants. The chocolate seemed to have disappeared, and what we had, looked and tasted remarkably like a little mound of tea-leaves. It seemed as though this was going to be something of a flop.

But that year we also happened to have in the long sequence of assorted creatures that at one time or another stayed with us – none of them were really pets – a budgerigar, given to us by a man who had recently retired from being a magician. This budgie had been trained to turn somer-saults on command. We learned the command, but we didn't know how to stop it, and the consequence of this latter-day Sorcerer's Apprentice story was that the budgie had balded itself in the corner of its cage, and had gone mental as any-thing. All that pent-up aggression was let loose on the tin of dried ants. It became the butcher bird of the budgie set, the condor of the kitchen. It seized ants and shook them, tossed them and snapped at them. Ant legs went one way, ant heads another – the carnage was worthy of Hogarth. It was the most ridiculous thing, a last hurrah as it turned out, for after that there didn't seem to be a lot of point in per-sisting with these gourmet novelties. They had been no more than diversions from the main course anyway.

So the day would drift through the long southern summer twilight into evening, and wind on to its approaching end, with everyone sitting around comfortably, or lolling on the floor, looking at each others' books, playing a new board game, listening to music, fiddling with the decorations on the tree. Sated with the social pleasure of Christmas. Looking back at ourselves all seated round about, *en famille*, we knew with absolute conviction that whatever rough beast was slouching towards Bethlehem, Yeats was at best describing a tendency; he was not yet right. And no, the modern era has not come to the end of history either, for this treasuring of custom keeps on leading us back into it. With time a family breaks up, which means that it re-arranges its parts, not that it breaks down – unless of course the parts are too idle to care. At its centre is amongst other things its recognition of whatever customs and traditions are significant for it, and which remain available to it. Custom is preserved only by the effort of maintaining it. As each generation follows the previous one, there are changes, but these are adjust-ments of approach, not of the value that inheres in custom itself: *plus ça change* ... Wisdom lies in discerning the patterns of signification, which is what custom and tradition offer us, both collectively and individually. It need not be onerous; it may be a very great pleasure. But like a cave painting, it has to be renewed again and again, maintained in order to preserve its virtue.

4

Taking the Country Air

(with William, and Mary)

The fifties and early sixties was a time when you could see exact divisions: the edges of things were clear. In days when people knew what was what, or thought they did, when the objection that something 'wasn't right' signalled a reinforcing of community values rather than their imminent collapse, and when hard currency was the only kind there was – in days before multiculturalism confused the self-evident truth of 'East is East and West is West, and ne'er the twain shall meet' – ours seemed a perfectly unambiguous, perfectly comprehensible world. This was a well-regulated because self-regulated community, regulated not by bull-dozed consensus or nimble contingency (which are no regulation at all), but by conviction. This was how things were done, or so we thought; this was the way we were.

At school, the boys played rough-and-tumble games like 'Red Rover, all over' and 'British Bulldog, one-two-three', stampeding from the galvanised iron fence at one side of the lower schoolyard to the picket fence at the other. They were always picking teams for games of this or that, and after school forming and re-forming into gangs with lurid names – the main activity of these coalitions seemed to consist in arguments about who else would or would not be let into the group. 'Whose side do you think you're on?' we would shout derisively at any unfortunate who, through a momentary lapse of concentration, was caught in the wrong place, seen going the wrong way. That was a thing you always kept your eye on, which way the flow was going. You had to keep your wits about you.

Closer to the class-rooms the girls played more contained games, skipping and knucklebones and statues, on the level asphalt area marked out in different coloured lines for netball, rounders and deck-tennis. And here at odd intervals in lesson time, classes would do something called marching. Fruity military airs burbled through large grey amplifiers at the corners of the bike-shed, and files of parodic children, all in different teams, marched along any of the lines, their chests thrown too far out, turning here or there at sharp right-angles, slyly engineering collisions with other files and vastly enjoying the sun and Sousa. 'Oh the maggots marched up Pitt Street with their boots on, and their hats on, and their pants on,' we sang under our breath, though nobody knew where Pitt Street might be. Nobody had travelled as far as Sydney; Melbourne was far enough. 'Bullshit, that's all the band could play; bullshit, they played it night and day . . .' We learned the clandestine words from uncles who had been to the war, and hadn't been impressed.

In class the desks were all in neat and exact rows. Across the blackboard, in a flawless round and unfaltering hand, the teacher had written a mnemonic: 'A place for everything, and everything in its place'. All was distinct, regular, real. There were columns of sums to do, ruled exercise books, text books with the correct answers printed towards the end. There were lists of words to memorise for spelling, and mental drill, speed and accuracy tests. Poetry was about listening to the metre:

By the shores of Gitche Gumee
By the shining Big-Sea-Water,
Stood the wigwam of Nokomis . . .

Music was about keeping time ('Watch my beat'). Education here was an exact discipline, its measure taken by the three-foot rule and a large pair of wooden compasses hanging from the blackboard ledge. The back cover of the ruled exercise books carried columns of measurement conversions: how many gills to a pint, how long a rod, pole or perch was, and how many of these to a furlong. How many pecks to a bushel. This information was never put to any use whatever, and not just because decimal conversion eventually made it redundant. It was never going to have any relevance. Which is no doubt why, perversely, we all remembered these things. They were remembered as curiosities.

Yet there were indolent times too, drowsy afternoons when the large mantel radio would be switched on and, slumped over our desks and our chin on our fore-arms, we learned about nature studies from Crosbie Morrison – while outside, on the abandoned marching area, inflamed pigeons strutted around one another with amorous intent, a thin-throated bantam rooster kept boasting unconvincingly from a backyard nearby, and kamikazi bees zoomed about the flowering gum next to the boys' toilet.

What did we do when school was out? What did we do in the holidays? Nothing much – we just mucked about. If it got really hot, Dads might take their family to the beach after work, to escape the mind-staggering heat of the suburbs for a few hours. Or perhaps that happened at the weekends, when we baked ourselves witless on the beach, listening, half drugged by the sun and the gentle slap of the waves, to radio broadcasts of Australia winning, splendidly, through the rounds of the Davis Cup yet again. And sometimes we might go for a holiday in the country.

That, come to think of it, must have been an adventurous undertaking, cars being what they were then, and roads being what they were then, and children being what they still are on trips – squirming and niggling, unsympathetic to whoever is feeling car-sick, endlessly complaining about not being able to see. The child is father to the man: nasty, brutish and short.

Everyone had connections in the country. Given that, and given the insistent cult of the bush in the Australian ethos, it is surprising how rarely any of us made a sortie into the heartland. Given that this could only happen in January, it is not surprising at all.

With the actual proximity of the country to the city, Patrick White's complaint that we were a nation of huddlers was demonstrably just. In Adelaide's case the demarcation was exorbitant. From the Hills, you could take a photograph of sheep grazing in the foreground, and the city spread across the plains below. To the north, the disjunction was even more pronounced. At what are called in American cartoons the city limits, on one side of the road was kerbing and the premise of a footpath, blistered letterboxes, a show of blotched and staggy roses, and brownish couch-grass lawns. On the other was a three-strand wire fence, with a row of topped gumtrees, and vast holding paddocks for sheep just brought down from the hinterland. Small white snails crowded up the seamed and splintering fenceposts, and even up whatever stubble was left. It all smelt dusty and rural and authentic. The city was just over here; the country started exactly there. And the road between, one of the few on the Adelaide plains with any sustained slope, was the site of the annual soapbox derby. Billycarts, Ginger Meggs and the Easterners used to call them; so, a downhill race for billycarts.

Across the road was the country, not 'the bush'. Likewise, for us it was people 'from the country' who wore the broad-brimmed, low-crowned hats at the Royal Show, not 'bushies'. Bushies were an affectation, whiskery creatures of myth, or perhaps from somewhere roughly in New South Wales. At this distance the catch-cry 'Sydney or the bush' was a fraudulent distinction, and in reality could only mean the hazard of no choice at all. The proper distinction was between Town and Country, as recognised in cricket matches and a long-established journal. The bush was nowhere, a figment of the romantic nationalistic imagination. But these were not considerations which concerned us then. We were going on a holiday in the country.

More precisely, we were going to stay at a little out-of-the-way place at the end of Yorke Peninsula, at a farm with its own beach. Perhaps there were other farms in the vicinity, but we did not notice them. We became completely caught up in where we were. So intense was our focus on the experience of each moment, so absorbed were we in whatever we were doing, that we had regard for no other. The days revolved around the fascinating here and now. The world or heaven lay about us: if we had any intimation of immortality, it rested in the complete irrelevance of time.

Peninsula people are, as anyone will tell you, different; and Corny Point is at its extremity, down long powdery roads dipping and rising and dipping again into the afternoon sun, past tumbledown limestone fences with rabbits sporting in and out of the holes in them, past long stretches of dusty ti-tree scrub and deserted bays where wrecked hulks rusted and sharks snoozed in the shallows of a shimmering grey and silent sea, past all this to the very end where granite reappears to pre-empt the shore, and where the countless rockpools and whitewashed lighthouse confirmed an unlikely

Enid Blyton setting for our games and adventures. There was nobody here but ourselves. For my brothers and myself, this did not feel like the end of anything, but rather the centre of everything. All our senses were quickened by our release into this new heaven, new earth.

Reflection provides understanding, but it does not alter the sense of what once we knew. It may even find a new shape in which to express the earlier experience. The poet Wordsworth, returning to Tintern Abbey, reacquainted himself with past associations and feelings, but came to a new understanding of how memory works. Remembering our early holidays we may do likewise, as also we may recognise how we reconstruct and re-create the past to suit a particular end. In my recollection, the important detail is the recognition that this was an experience of heightened awareness, one of those spots of time when time might scarcely be, and somehow brought home to us, even while we were in the midst of it.

To begin with, there was the rich store of the farm itself. Farms and farm animals we all know about from nursery rhymes and stories, and that familiarity was, at first glance, confirmed. But soon our senses became more subtly attuned to it. Here was an enclave seemingly sealed off from the rest of the world, sheltered in behind the sandhills from the prevailing breeze. Big glorious summer clouds floated high overhead. Nothing seemed to actually happen here: an old horse stood patiently in a paddock near the shed, flinching to shake off flies. A rusting windmill creaked slowly, and only a little water dribbled out into the trough, where strands of mossy weed wavered, and galahs perched unconfidently on the edge to drink. A solitary crow groaned from a big sheoak, and the shed's galvanised iron roof ticked in the sun. Everything was entranced, though not waiting for anything in particular.

Inside the shed were bits and pieces of everything, leather straps and buckles, old tools, grindstones and pitchforks, hand shears and rabbit traps, strange machinery, lengths of wire, bags of chaff, and a loft full of cobwebs; and all fermenting into a rich heady mix of smells, of mice and dust and grain and oil. No doubt there had been parental instruction, but you did not need to touch. You took it all in, silently, standing on the patch of worn and stained earth at the entrance; then you went off to swish at the mallow weeds with a stick, and to poke at old forgotten bantam eggs under them.

The stone farm-house nestled in a hollow. The blond paddocks stopped at a low limestone wall mortared together but cracking apart, and an ancient box-thorn hedge; a picket gate had long since given up keeping the bantams out of the desiccated garden. Water is a precious commodity in this country. Scratchy lavender bushes marked out a kind of path, and piece-rate worker bees hovered about them, trying to do a head-count. Pigeons preened and strutted on the roof-top, until chased off just before mealtimes by the new shift of silver gulls.

I do not recall much of what the house itself was like: for some reason it appears to have made very little impression on me. The recollection of mere detail, retrieved fact, memory of the pick-a-box sort, is of virtually no interest. Some further intimation has to come with it. Only those details which made their mark can have informed the mind's discerning eye, and lend a certain notional shape to what was then perceived, until memory's kaleidoscope brings it once more into focus, or near enough for contemplation.

There was an old wind-up record-player with a massive head and sharpened bamboo needle, and not a lot of records – the Mississippi Waltz, and a comic skit about a German carpenter, the point of which remained elusive to us. The ceilings were honey-coloured pine planks, with dried seaweed above them for insulation, and at night the rooms ripened in the soft yellow 32-volt light from the Freelite wind generator. All was snug and Peggotty-ish.

I slept in what used to be the shearers' quarters, at the back of the house. Here the walls were white-washed, but with the same pine ceilings, and a pinewood cupboard, and just outside the door a smallish haystack, honey-coloured too, but which loomed large and silver in the moonlight. The cupboard contained a mystery: from it came a strong, choking, sweetish smell, and an unvarying droning note, not near nor far, nor angry nor joyous, no barbarous 'ou-boom' nor nature playing an untuned Aeolian harp. I had, all to myself, a cupboard full of lavender-feeding bees. Martin Boyd said we romanticise whatever interests us, but he may have been thinking of something else; this clearly had the wrong kind of interest, or not enough romantic distance. Yet when the bees settled, and I settled, I could hear soft chitterings from the hedge, and the distant wash of the waves, and knew the moon shone on them, and dreamed I slept in a honey-coloured sea cave.

The farm had been settled and the house built by an old German family. Now only one son, a widower, and his sister, a spinster, both elderly in their turn, remained to carry on the family farm, with the help of a share-farmer. Neither was reclusive, yet both were absorbed in their own mysteries – for Walter was a diviner, and Mary was wise in the ways of the sea. Walter was large and wore braces, and filled out the back of his brown trousers. Mary was slender and had the deep-set, watchful eyes one associates with deaf people: Henry Lawson eyes, only light blue. She had fair powdery skin, and faded rosy cheeks, and a gentle, musing manner.

They were generous and hospitable and discreet. They did not speak about themselves, or about the difficulties their family had faced over the many years. They were of the country, and observed the courtesies of the country way of life: there was nothing of the bush about them. I heard a story later that in the lean times of earlier years Mary had, as a treat for the family, laboriously gleaned the berries from the box-thorn bushes, and made a tart, and put it on the kitchen window sill to cool; and when she came to serve up her surprise, the filling had all disappeared. She was vexed, she was distressed, she accused her brothers of being selfish and eating it, it wasn't fair, they were making fun of her, they were teasing her, tormenting her. They sat silent at the table through it all, big men; and later that afternoon they brought her another bowl of berries, all washed, and she made another tart, though she couldn't think where there were any other bushes. The next day she found a large lizard in the garden, its belly cut open.

That story fascinates me. It has distinct Steele Rudd possibilities. Like so many bush yarns, it speaks of marginal subsistence and an almost grotesque sardonicism. It feels apocryphal. And there is a fairy-tale aspect to it too, part Cinderella, the put-upon drudging youngest, the unappreciated gift of the mute princess-to-be, or in this case the deaf but engagingly fair sister, German romantic legend reappearing in this most unlikely outreach ... Yet it is the other aspect that my mind turns to: did the brothers have difficulty eating the second tart? What would the recycled pie taste like? How did they feel when Mary thanked them? What would Mary have been able to say to them on the next day? Pale echoes of the undeclared voices hung in the pinewood ceiling. Country discretions, when they become stated, descend into the farcical brutality of the bush ethos.

I cannot think that Walter would have gone berry-picking or lizard-hunting: he wasn't the type. Although by the time we went to stay there he had retired, he would still go off to the mallee scrub and cut fence-posts all morning. I cannot imagine he removed his hat or waistcoat either. He hitched up the jinker: the horse stood mouthing her bit and shaking her head and making the traces jingle while he loaded on axes and a thermos of tea and some rolled up papers and a hessian bag or two. Then off we went, over a cattle grid and down a pale grassy track and on through a sequence of wire gates; the horse settled down to a steady pace, occasionally breaking wind and knocking one of her hooves against another. The smooth rubber tyres burred over the sandy track – it followed across the back of ancient dunes, dipping through hollows and shallow rises and into a surprising stand of nevertheless small trees. Magpies were calling, rabbits sat up in bald patches between low bushes and watched us pass. The air had a tang, of dried grass, wind drift and spume; the paddocks vibrated in the sun.

Soon we came to a defeated-looking old drilling rig balanced on the back of a scrapheap truck. A scraggy character was sinking a well; he had been at it for a week or so in that place and it didn't look too promising, so Walter had been called in. Walter spoke for a bit to the man, checked the maps he had brought with him, and then got out his divining rod, which looked pretty much like the centre of a bicycle pedal with a long slender metal rod through one end. He held it with a special stone in his huge fist and – squeezed? waited? concentrated? repeated some mystic incantation? Whatever it was, nothing happened, and he moved twenty or so paces along the slope of the hollow. Slowly the point swung around, and he counted: water at seven hundred feet! Walter was held in great esteem, or at least locally. It was said he could divine for minerals by suspending a weight on a string over a geological survey map. So, water there would be.

Then it was my turn. The stone was a piece of limestone about the size of a golf-ball, hollow, with a black spot on it. He put that and the pedal thing in my hand, and wrapped his great thick fingers around mine – and slowly the pointer swung around. He let go, and still it swung round, steadily and strongly: five-six-seven, and stopped. That did not seem to surprise him, but it thrilled me; yet I did not feel I could speak of it to him. It had moved for me! It worked for me! As I recall it, what I felt then was not a matter of sensation, but of privilege, and awe. I was indifferent to my brothers' subsequent taunts, that I had been pretending. I had something else to think about now, and their envy seemed to fall a long way from me.

We drove back to the farmhouse. I was absorbed in the mood of this moment, almost suspended in it. The susurrus of the tyres on the grass and sandy track, the furry splinters in the tray of the jinker, the creak and the smell – almost the taste – of the wire loops that held the gates closed, the marram grass and windburnt bushes, the muffled flat thud of the sea, all these were parts of a world which was not my own, yet which contented me very well. And now, in a way I did not understand, it had made contact with me, it had told me something about itself.

With Mary, we walked down a path through the sandhills to the beach. She would point out the succulents safe to eat – not only point them out, but insist we try them then and there. They were so salt and bitter we were sure she had made a mistake.

The lighthouse close up was uninteresting. It was cracked, it needed painting; but also it was too big, too big to meet anything like the idea of it. Such a romantic figure requires a certain distance for the reach of the imagination. The mind cannot embrace the meaning of it when it is abruptly immediate and merely real. Even Wordsworth had had to back off a little from his mountain peaks and waterfalls, in time if not in space, rightly to envisage and envision them.

At the top of the beach everything had a pungent scurf of salt – granite boulders, grey splintered timbers washed up on a high tide, tangles of dried seaweed and sea-wrack. Further down was a reef of shells, ten thousand at a glance, all kinds and shapes of shells, minute fan shells yellow, orange, red, brown, black, mother-of-pearl, broken nautilus, cockles, spirals, cuttlefish. Sometimes we would find a dead baby shark, and we were ambitious of finding a beached whale. The skeleton of the great whale in the South Australian museum was said to have come from the farm beach, and Mary had also found a shell that was named after her. There was always the chance that you might find something really interesting here.

So we drifted along the beach, in short-legged khaki overalls and fading blue cotton sou-westers, peering into rockpools, enticing crabs with some shellfish meat on a piece of string, flipping starfish over and poking at anemones, making small boats out of cuttlefish shells and seagull feathers. The sun beat down on a flattened sea, the small waves flopped casually on the shell-grit shingle, the water sucked and gurgled in and out of the rockpools. The sounds all seemed to come from far off: it was the hushed suspension of midsummer noon in the great Australian outdoors.

On one occasion we collected periwinkles. Mary had brought a kerosene-tin bucket, and we were all put to work. In no time we had half the tin filled, which she thought might be enough, and we had a pile of driftwood. The periwinkles were set to boil in seawater, and then she tried to persuade us to eat them. But we could not. They were no more tempting than the pigface. There were too many of them. And we tried not to think that we had seen their trails wandering unhappily across smooth patches of sand in the bottom of the rockpools. Besides, she was prising out the meat with a bobbypin she had taken from her hair, and I for one had suddenly become finicky. But we didn't mind putting the little round gritty lids on our nose or on our cheeks – and depending on how many stayed in place, we must sometimes have looked as if we had beauty spots, and sometimes the pox.

Here, under a bright and vibrant sky, in all the vast quietude of this sea-verge, and in a dissolving mood of relaxed receptivity, as I understand it now, it was possible to retrieve what Wordsworth called a primal sympathy. Here was a kind of large elemental balance, which I certainly felt, but could not then have identified. The constituent features of all this world, or as much of it as you could see at the very end of Yorke Peninsula, were all held in balance, all checked by each other. For example, in spite of the significance of the lighthouse, and the story of the whale skeleton (the skeleton certainly existed), and the heavy timbers high up on the beach, and the dead baby shark drowned at sea as I imagined, all the present evidence of our senses, and the certainty of endless new discoveries to be made, and the conviction that this was a haven for us, all denied the possibility of storms. Those belonged to another season, but this by our experience was manifestly a place of eternal season, always summer, stormless. The signs were impotent, silent; they did not speak to us.

The tempting Wordsworthian response cannot however be sustained, for this was not the vision splendid, nor nature's holiday. For one thing, these weren't mighty waters rolling evermore: if anything, they were suspended in disbelief. Here was a landscape, taking that term in its widest sense, devoid of moral force, because it had no meaning, no design for us, beyond the direct experience of it. This was a silent sea; the vibrancy of the sky betokened not an animating principle, but a kind of register of delight, primal delight.

The farm, sheltering behind the dunes, seemed complete in itself, but it was always in opposition to the seascape. It was therefore slightly out of balance, when you thought about it in relation to the coast it nestled against. Curiously, Australian writers rarely bring their images of the country into conjunction with the sea. When that does happen the romantic myth of the bush is suddenly confronted by a new imaginative dimension, and discovered to have an under-lying insufficiency, even a kind of hollowness – as in say Henry Handel Richardson's *The Getting of Wisdom*, or the last phase of *The Fortunes of Richard Mahony*. In the Cape Furze episode of *Lucinda Brayford*, Martin Boyd powerfully revises the estimation of the Australian countryside and identifies it as essentially pagan. In that sparse and windswept headland, he traced out an affinity between Australia and the Mediterranean not just by comparison with the classical landscape, but also by the 'pagan' spirit that informs the place-sense – the 'something far more deeply interfused'. One thinks, for example, of say Cape Sounion in Greece, with its frank congruence of the primal elements – sky, sea, land, each declared in the full force of its simplicity of form, and meeting at that point. So forceful is the point of inter-section that the temple there seems to lift, to be the very manifestation of the pagan or classical spirit (Byron's carved signature being neither of those, but barbarity), and not just the expression of it.

At Cape Furze, or Corny Point, or at many other locations around Australia, the same perception can be made. Yet Australia is still largely unperceived. Things of the spirit are unrecognised, unattempted. Here, on that holiday, were sky, sea, land, and the absence of anything else; and the very absence contributed to the remembered potency of their interaction. Memory is what enables the integration, memory discovers the means of bringing them together. In memory is discovered the principle of unity. In this sense it is the mind that, half creating, half perceiving, permits the pleasure of recognition – not of things seen distinct in themselves, not of exact divisions but, as we are later convinced, of their true relations to each other. The rational mind teaches us some things, but the processes of memory confirm the relation of our feelings to moral sentiments; and that is a kind of knowledge that could do with more airing in our country.

5

On the Plains of Clay

There are only two jokes about Adelaide. The Cousin Jack jokes from the old Cornish community at the Moonta and Kadina copperfields don't count, for they are about a particular cultural sub-set. The first, that Adelaide was laid out in 1836, never to rise again, I've already tried out on you. The other is that the dead centre of Adelaide, all four-square and symmetrical, is at West Terrace. Any further comment is uncalled for.

Not that South Australia is a lugubrious community. There are after all only those two funereal jokes. From the first days of colonisation, death lay all about, but somehow the high Victorian preoccupation of the day with death did not convince. Our beginnings were brought together with our endings into a firm circle, for the city fathers planned for our mortal taking off as carefully as they did to establish a moral new society, in setting aside ample burial grounds adjacent to the city boundary. Institutionalised, if set off to one side, the deathly was somehow under control. The proprieties would be observed from the very beginning. Adelaide was, significantly, built on plains of clay, constant reminder of whence we must return, constant trial of my father's patience as he tried to dig over the garden.

For generations to come, the evidence of ring-barked trees, sun-burned paddocks and immense bushfires through the Adelaide Hills, dust-storms coming in from the north, or locust plagues, made the insistent presence of death and destruction familiar, familiarised us with that, and became emblems of a way of life. Beyond the Goyder line – the indicative line drawn on the state map by a sensible surveyor general, beyond which he said it was inadvisable to establish anything like permanent settlement, a kind of *ne plus ultra* – the terrain was, still is, dotted with crumbling limestone walls and sturdier chimneys, the ruins of settlers' dreams. Goyder was right, and is still ignored. At its most extreme, in the desert interior of the north of the state, Charles Sturt trespassed into a country beyond death, where the corpses of cattle did not putrefy. In this colony in particular, it was as though death did not have its customary sting, for like the way of life, so the way of death was somehow at a remove, and as I have been arguing in these essays, it is like everything else in South Australia, experienced (though in this case, of course) at a distance. Yet for all its reputation as having a dry and ungenerous climate, even if the South Australian soil is not up to scratch and we grew whichever way we would, it must have nourished us, for we did in fact grow. And we grew without really trying. We were like the famed roses. We were an introduced species that did very well; especially in the suburbs.

This was a time for growth. Our parents might not have forgotten the difficult times before and during the war. We could remember only a few of the direct effects – a filled-in air-raid trench in the back garden which was the cradle for enormous parsnips. King-sized, my father said proudly. The only king I knew of was hollow-cheeked King George, parsnip-coloured as far as we could translate from the black-and-white Movietone News at the Saturday afternoon matinees. Why Adelaide needed air-raid trenches was never satisfactorily explained. Enemy aircraft would have run out of fuel long before they could return to their bases from a raid. But if we were going to be in the war, we had to do it properly. That was a Richmal Crompton kind of argument. There were petrol and clothing coupons, and building restrictions, though historians like to persuade us this was an era of national reconstruction. I have a vague visual memory of the butcher clipping a diagonal half of a rectangle from a booklet of ration coupons, and my father preserved a book of petrol coupons, testimony to one of the few occasions in his life when he was 'privileged'. Aunts still knitted us cable-stitch jumpers and sleeveless pullovers – only actors in ABC costume dramas think anyone actually dressed like Ginger Meggs, in diamond patterned designs; beneficiaries of a different set of aunties.

That post-war era was still a time for making do, for women to exchange jars of jams and preserves, for men to grow their own vegetables and keep chooks and re-sole shoes, for us to make our own fun, refurbish our own things. We sanded down and repainted our own bikes, taught the cocky to swear, visited neighbours to see their zebra finches, listened to Spike Jones on someone else's new 78 rpm electric gramophone, and stockpiled Captain Marvel and Phantom ('the ghost who walks') comics under the bed, next to the box of home-made puppets where the cat had her kittens one famous year. Kapow! Crunch! and the forces of good spifflicated sinister agents of destruction left, right and centre. In more modern self-consciously ironic readings it would be understood they must mainly be of the left ... (How Blackhawk's 'hawk-a-a-a-ah' must have put the wind up those terrible commies!)

It was, famously, a time for cricket in the back yard; inter-estingly, not in the street. You played footie in the street, and only the best kicks managed to make it over the elec-tricity lines draped from the telegraph posts – these slowly being replaced by stobie poles right throughout the suburbs. There must have been telephone wires too, but not very many of these to begin with. Whatever had happened in the war was a very long way away. There were Legacy kids and dawn services at the memorial in the council gardens, where the long white angels' trumpets of the datura swung, enticing and poisonous alongside the playground. It was the rumour of their deadliness that attracted us, not any possible association with their common name. The names of things rarely held any significance. Words and events had to acquire their own meaning. Anzac meant the Gallipoli landing and a holiday. Anzac Parade already meant a main road, not a contingent of returned soldiers, and Memorial Gardens meant playgrounds and beds of roses. Memorial Drive meant Sedgman and McGregor, and then Hoad and Rosewall, serving it up to the Yanks, belting scorching passing shots up the tramlines. Kapow! Crunch! And roses outside the chainwire boundaries of the tennis court precinct, roses, roses all the way.

It was still an age innocent of the sensitivities that came with consciousness-raising and then later again, political correctness, a time when children had golliwogs and sang 'Ten little nigger boys' without embarrassment. Maybe Coon cheese got marketed at about the same time. There were of course occasions of snickering, but it was pretty harmless. For example, when we had tired of the uncertainties of Snakes and Ladders, and the gridlock frustrations of Chinese Chequers played with brightly painted quondongs, we would likely enough resort to Hang the Butcher. Someone thinks of a word, and you have to guess letter by letter what it is. For each letter that is wrong, a bit more of the scaffold, rope, body of the hanging man gets drawn in, with ultimate defeat when the legs are added to dance on the air. As is the way with any game, certain strategies inevitably evolved. Go for the vowels first. To counter that manoeuvre we developed an unlikely vocabulary – crypt, tryst, myrrh. We agreed that long words were not allowed, as the gallows would be up, the rope thrown, and the sagging butcher past his last paroxysm (another useful word) well before the whole of 'unconsciousness' could be worked out – or my mother's favourite, 'antidisestablishmentarianism'. Whatever that meant. It was easy enough to recognise in the abstract.

All over the house were scraps of paper with partly or entirely executed butchers. Why butchers? There was no anxiety about that. You just hanged them. This was a game about vocabulary, not moral sensibility. It was also a means of trapping the unwary. We set temptation in the way of the less uninnocent, kids from up and down the street, by setting words like shut, cork, tuck. Their eyes would open wide as they hesitated before what they thought they recognised. I don't suppose we left those tell-tale scraps of evidence lying about the house.

We played with death and we played at death. It didn't mean anything. After all, like most children we had been brought up with the gruesome if not gory: Little Red Riding Hood, Jack the Giant-Killer, the Three Little Pigs. We weren't going to be easily upset by ideas of the morbid or violent. Boys took pot-shots at each other from around corners, set ambushes, charged and yelled, 'Got you! You're dead!' We played a fierce game of brandy, throwing a balding tennis ball as hard as we could right at someone; the tell-tale red marks on our arms and legs explained the name.

The girls, being sissies, played at statues. We lobbed bombs at each other, weeds with a clump of dirt still attached to the roots.

At the Royal Show there was a difficult choice about what to see first. Perhaps the Globe of Death, a mesh sphere inside which motorcyclists looped over and over each other, faster and closer and faster still, their exhausts sounding like machine guns, and round and round but never quite crashing into each other. Nearly though; that was all the thrill we were going to get from that. You could take a turn at being pinned against the Wall of Death – like standing inside a vast and yet to become commonplace spin-dryer. As it went round faster and faster, so you slowly started to rise up the wall; and you could only look at the person directly opposite, you hardly dared swivel your eyeballs. Or you could ride the Ghost Train, lurching and twisting through long dark tunnels, and at the very end a skeleton stepping out to touch us; and the toughest kids stood up and punched the skeleton as hard as they could in an invisible midriff; and sometimes we got to hear an anguished word from Hang the Butcher. We stood up to death; well, the tough kids did. The rest of us, more cautious if not apprehensive, looked on, and the train bumped and juddered and swung tight around to the left and just as it appeared to crash into a brick wall we were out in the daylight world again. And that was all the thrill we were going to get from that too.

So when death made its first momentous impact, almost inevitably it happened in the midst of carnival. Throughout the summer months, crowds thronged to the beaches to set up an early disposition to melanoma, not that we knew anything of that, but also in the evenings to join the amusements of the sideshows, the hurdy gurdy, the boxing tent, and the council band pumping away in the rotunda. There were squeals from the ferris-wheel, raucous huckstering from the hoopla stall, the thwack of wooden balls against the canvas back of the skittles alley, the crack of airguns and occasionally a tinny ding as a duck got knocked over. 'Righteo, who'll 'ave a go? Every shot's a winner! Roll up, roll up!' – why roll? They were strong hectoring voices, carrying over the din, the same sort of voices as at the vegetable markets and fishmarkets, not inviting but bullying. A line of disconsolate men stood on a platform outside the tent advertising Jim Sharman's Boxing Troupe. 'Who'll try themselves tonight? Come on come on. A pound or two for a round or two.' And invariably it was someone who had already had a round or two in the hotel across the road that put up his reckless hand, and got a walloping. There wasn't much pleasure in watching a beefy man's flabby torso turned by degrees rosier and rosier; the pink watery blood smearing across his upper lip was disgusting because pathetic. For the pro, a disdainful Aboriginal though the identification hardly registered with us in those days, it was all too easy. The thud of his gloves on the rapidly sobering challenger wasn't as convincing as the balls whacking into the canvas sheet behind the skittles, a sound that carried into the boxing tent.

And then suddenly, an announcement over the public address system. The parsnip king from over the seas had died. Somehow this news broke an elusive connection. For years we had been required to eat up all our vegetables, as though that somehow contributed to the general fibre of England at large, and more particularly to its starving children who we were required to think of along with the Brussels sprouts and spinach – 'Eat up, think of the starving millions in England'. Yet England's king, and ours, had faded away. An old order had not just passed, it had somehow fallen apart, like a stack of skittles; and the carnival was over. The band played the national anthem, meaning 'God Save the King', though that was a puzzle, and God was too late. From now on it would be the new young Queen who needed watching out for. People began drifting away, as though they had been caught out having an inappropriate good time; they had been careless of his ill-health. Fishermen appeared out of the dark, coming in from the long unlit jetty with their small catches of tommy ruff. Soon the lights at the swimming pool ('the baths') were turned off, and then the lights on the abandoned ferris wheel, and the hurdy-gurdy, where the riderless glossy horses had started to look frantic. The fish and chip shop stayed open for a bit, but with no customers the altered state of affairs asserted itself there too. Soon the night was left to the curling waves rolling in from the outer darkness, their creaming edges just catching the pale light thrown by the streetlights along the empty Esplanade, and shadowed by the row of large Norfolk Island pines. Nothing looked emptier than the rotunda. It seems to me now that it was never used again.

We talked about all this in the dark, my brothers and I, in our beds where we were staying at our grandparents' house. For the first time we were attempting to make sense of something both big and remote. We were trying to guess at what it would mean for us, what might be different. What had changed was ourselves; we had become aware of change, aware that change could happen. The hermetically sealed provincial world of what was to that point pretty much a colony in its attitudes had had its day, its long day in the sun. We had become connected to something much larger than ourselves, even though in our provincial way we had always assumed that connection as a birth-right.

The moment of connection was a moment of rupture;

we would have a different self to become acquainted with after this. Where could we see change? The gold initials on the bright red pillar boxes for starters, new postage stamps. Currency would begin soon enough to be re-designed; change was the new order of the day. Timelessness, our birthright, would survive only as an illusion; timelessness, and with it that reassuring inner conviction of something like immortality. So we began to pay attention, to statues and commemorative issues, to the family plot in the Payneham cemetery (out along the tramline to Paradise), to the deaths of explorers rather than their pointless discoveries: death was the legacy of history. But still, as with sad King George, death was at a distance, and dignified by that distance. And death was not finality, it was change.

The evidence of change was dramatic, when a year later a huge coastal storm wrecked the jetties and the baths, disinterred great reefs of last season's rotting seaweed, winter wrack. The huge seas broke up the sea wall and washed away the road and the sand and rubble behind it. With the sea wall went the 'caves' built into it, and their red and yellow picket fences, places which the older resident families owned, or held on a long lease, and where they had kept their deckchairs and other beach paraphernalia. With the jetty went a servery at beach level immediately beneath it, where you used to get hot water for the necessary cup of tea. The storm lay waste to more than the grey stuccoed concrete walls, and the huge Norfolk Island pines, and a curious fishpond with an ugly central column and arabesque patterns on its tiles; it washed away an older, genteel beach culture. In came sun-baking and beach-tennis and portable radios. The storm ravaged the surviving sand-hills and clogged up the mouth of the Torrens, and the fine white sand turned a dirty pale grey colour. In the redevelopment which followed, boarding houses gave way to blocks of flats. The railway line was closed, then the tramline; and it wasn't the same going to the beach by bus.

And change was precipitate, meaning not only that it came suddenly and swiftly, but that when it came it changed things utterly. We shifted house. One morning I went to school, leaving the parsnip bed and the loquat tree and the gap through the fence to Parsons' house, and after school walked a new route to a new home. Familiarity had relocated – the cat and her three kittens had taken up residence, and the chooks were in a new, old chook run, and the kitchen was full of familiar clutter but with a brand new laminex and chrome table replacing the old pine kitchen table (did it have a dark green linoleum surface? I can't remember, but the new one was a patterned lettuce green). We had our own mats and candlewick bedspreads, our clothes were in our own wardrobes ... but that relocated world, while it would become the chief ground of my remembering, itself underwent on-going embellishment. We would get new bedspreads, built-in cupboards, bikes. We got a new telephone, a big chunky bakelite set sitting on a kidney shaped table with a shelf for the directory, the telephone book. We started a new vegetable garden.

The soil was good and dark, the garden beds had been well dug over by the previous owners; and over the years my father would continue to dig chook manure from the laying shed and work it into the beds of potatoes, beans, pumpkins, sweetcorn and, yes, parsnips; and next to the beans another trellis for sweet peas. We had fruit trees and grapevines and almond trees; we had a small squad of ducks to keep down the snails, and a few bantams for no good at all, and a galah and a tame magpie, and from time to time we kept a rabbit. And we had cats. We had cats and we had kittens and before they were really big enough they were having kittens and in no time flat we were over-run by cats and kittens. Dr Seuss's solution would have been to get a dog. Dr Seuss had yet to be invented, and my unhappy father was required to do something about it. He was the kind of man who just before Christmas would catch one of the older chooks or ducks, there would be a flurry of squawks or quacks and flapping wings and a small cloud of feathers – we were not allowed to watch all this action – and then clunk, the axe thumped into the chopping block and my father would hand over to my mother the makings for Christmas dinner and lie down on his bed for the rest of the afternoon. So the cat solution was particularly hard on him. As also on the cat.

One of the second generation of cats was 'put down'. Don't ask. Definitely not a hatchet job. And it was buried somewhere in amongst the vegetables – he was a man of feeling, but having made his way through the Depression, for him sentiment could always be tempered by an awareness of possible economy. This time, instead of taking to his bed he took to the garden, digging and weeding and pruning and filling up his barrow with things to throw on the mound of rubbish at the far end of the garden. He turned, and saw a very draggled cat digging its way backwards out of the vegetable patch, its wet fur clogged with the rich earth … and that was quite enough for him for that afternoon.

We of course thought it was hysterically funny. Well, so it was. Straight out of 'Dad and Dave'. It was also a further marker of our progressive loss of innocence. The cat had other lives to lead, but an assortment of chickens, ducklings, the rabbit (heat exhaustion probably, but we wondered uneasily whether 'myxie' had made its way into the suburbs, jumping our galvanised iron fence), creatures great and small on their way to their maker found a convenient waiting room in shallow graves under the lemon tree, where nothing much grew.

The chief celebrant was my cousin, come to stay with us for an undeclared length of time. His mother had recently died of meningitis; his no-good unseen father was nowhere to be seen, probably back in prison, where in my mind he served a life sentence, somehow in full Highland regalia and with bagpipes. So my cousin came to stay a while, and as he was close to my age, just a little older, I was to be especially caring of him. He didn't go to school but he came each afternoon to wait for me at the school gate, sent no doubt by my mother to give him something to do, and on our way home he would watch out for dead pigeons, dead sparrows, dead anything so that he could bury them under the lemon tree; giving himself something to do. He was fascinated not so much by corpses as by interment. He loved scraping out the little hollows, and dumping the body, and mounding up the earth over it. The correlation with his mother's funeral is too obvious. I think his enthusiasms were his own, and peculiar. He would go fossicking up forbidden lanes, in amongst the clumps of long grass on undeveloped blocks, trawling through streets beyond the route home; and because I was meant to be looking after him I had to go with him. He had me not so much in tow as in thrall; I had been awaited, collected, and I no longer had freedom to choose what to do. I had been shanghaied right beneath my parents' eyes, annexed. When I tried to explain my uneasiness I was enjoined to be more understanding. It felt like being the entangled body in a spider's web. I was the horrified witness to what was happening to me, and there was nothing I could do about it.

Towards Guy Fawkes Day everyone counted up their pocket money and debated what was the best range of fireworks to buy with that amount. My cousin may have had some pocket money, but he quickly had a lot more fireworks than seemed accountable. And in a very short time I was being shown how he did it, pinching crackers from the local newsagency – he had inherited more than a disposition to bagpipes from his fast-fingered father. To be shown is to be compromised. The next moment, impatient with my stupidity in just standing there, holding the merchandise, he was shoving roman candles and catharine wheels down the front of my jumper, and a Mt Vesuvius in my pocket; he had already loaded up his own. And then he was nudging me out of the shop and now I was a terrified accessory.

Not so terrified though as I was that night, in the sleep-out he was sharing with me. With the lights out and the house settling down to quietness, he leaned across out of his bed and put the matter directly to me: 'Don't you tell.'

He must have read my uneasiness; he couldn't have had much confidence in my acquiescence. In two quick steps, Highlander steps, he was choking me. No, that phrase is too matter of fact. He was crushing my throat. And what I resented – what *offended* me – was that he was making my throat hurt, bruising something; crushing a lump in my throat, making me gag, making me want to hawk up and yet the crushing wouldn't let the convulsing happen, and all I could feel was bitterness. This wasn't my doing, this wasn't my fault, this was unfair. This was my own first cousin, almost my own age. And I reviled him, hated him, and couldn't spit it out.

And more offensive again, he was playing with me. Not playing at strangling me. Playing with me as victim. This was playing! His grip eased, and then he bore down again, and then eased again. My Adam's apple was crushed – okay, severely bruised. Would the bruise turn soft and brown, the bit you wanted to spit out? Would its rot spread? 'If you say anything I'll finish you off.' This, this shocking, no this outrageous wrenching, dislocating, separating act, in my house, my room, my bed, my place, was just that, an act, merely an act. The first act. And he was taking over my place from me, not just my breath. I had never encountered such brutality, I didn't know how you were meant to behave in relation to it, how you accommodated it. It was already here, under the family roof. The shock was not so much to me as to my upset sense of what the world, the small world I had grown up in, could contain. I wouldn't say anything. I couldn't.

Nothing happened. Nothing ever happens. No exploding parent crashed into the room and pointed an accusing finger. No nick of time salvation of the good. Natural justice was conspicuously in abeyance. And no reparations, as it turned out, in the days that followed. I wasn't brave enough to weep, under the strict surveillance of my cousin, closer to me now than ever, to call attention to my injured self. The nights were a torment, lying anxiously in the dark, listening to any movement he might make, anxious to make none myself. I was the stunned prey swivelling in the cobweb. I was miserable, with a lie locked in my throat.

Yet we do find ways of reconciling ourselves to the world – indeed, we must, or we couldn't endure it. So there was a certain satisfaction that my parents were at some stage puzzled by the quantity of crackers we let off that Guy Fawkes Day, and that was enquired into, and there was mutual recrimination because I was relieved at last to be able to tell a whole truth for once. And there was another satisfaction in the words we used to chant at that time of the year, about that obscure Hang the Butcher figure from a history that had nothing to do with us:

Guy Guy Guy
Stick him up high
String him from a lamp post
And there let him die.

What I knew, or rather felt, was that all this had nothing to do with *me*. It wasn't connected with me, even though – even while – it was happening to me. I did not consent to this, it was not an event which at the most important level involved me. Shock and rage hardened into absolute resistance. I rejected all this. And that. And him.

He returned to our grandparents soon after that (perhaps my parents were more observant than I realised?) and I suppose lived there for a bit, and probably dug holes beneath their lemon tree. As far as I know I have never seen him again, not even to dream of. But he did return once to our collective attention, years afterwards, when the grandfather we all shared died. The funeral service had been conducted with the usual awkwardnesses and emotional strains, absences were noticed including my own and that of my cousin, the older generation were circling unhappily about the open grave when, as my brother reported later, a noisy ute roared up to the cemetery, trailing its own cloud of choking dust and fumes, the windscreen too dirty to see through – and out jumped my cousin in tam and kilt, reached into the cabin for his pipes and then began screeling something which resembled 'Amazing Grace' more than anything else.

I imagine this scene strongly, the outlandish sound in a suburban cemetery, the hard fingers of the strangler pressing on the chanter. The stunned relatives forgot for a moment their grieving, gaping at this apparition from literally the other side of the grave, who began pacing restlessly and intently between the mounds and headstones. No Scotsman, no antipodean imitation Scot, can stand still while playing the pipes it seems – or perhaps it was a habit acquired from hours of practice in the backblocks, relocating himself from time to time from the forensic anger of bull-ants. It was unnecessary in this instance, given that curious characteristic of suburban cemeteries, a dearth of ants. Perhaps ants are discouraged as in poor taste. It occurs to me that given the clay and limestone rubble so characteristic of South Australia, it would be hard going for worms too. With a skirl and a flourish, grace was allowed to suspire and he withdrew in the same rampaging disorder, threw his collapsed pipes back into the cabin, gunned the motor and headed off back to the interior. Dust to dust.

No doubt everyone has a comparable experience of some such kind of violent intrusion in those years of early adolescence, a violation not so much of the person but a betrayal of what we thought of as the shape of our world. It is an order of experience which there is little point in revisiting, other than as a kind of self-indulgence; or, my excuse here, as an example. Nothing gets changed by these exhumations. Emotionally, we shrug. The meek are not going to inherit the earth. Yet it seems to me these sorts of episodes confirm early for us our convictions about what is right and wrong, our notions of what is good or bad. That's a knowledge that comes instantly, not by thinking upon the event. Through such experiences we find ourselves in direct contact with a deeply residual conviction of natural justice, or more precisely, injustice. Through such minor catastrophes, though we might rate them more seriously at the time, we identify the values which we will continue to hold in high regard. Similarly, bit by bit we learn the absolute exclusivity of the private self; and of course its corollary, the relative unimportance of the individual. That's probably no longer a popular notion. Perhaps in a different culture we might have been better prepared for sardonicism. This was still an innocent age and an innocent community, the subsequent and still inexplicable disappearance of the Beaumont children notwithstanding. One way or another, and one by one, we were being tested and found wanting; and all we could do was retreat to a kind of suburban fatalism, if not stoicism. Our only choice evidently was in the degree of tenacity with which we would sustain it. Endurance vile. What, when all was said and done, was the damage? And who would want to hear your story when they all had their own? The lesson that was reinforced was that not only were we left out of our national history, but also out of our own history. Some years later, in a phrase written at the end of a French assignment I had handed in at University, I thought I had come across an enigmatic formulation of what this had all meant for me: '*Cela m'est égal*'. It chimed with both my mood and my limited comprehension. It is a phrase that I long continued to turn over and over, like a piece of chewing gum, until it too lost its savour.

The ceremonies of death, the observances associated with all this final leave-taking, came to seem unequal to the occasion, that is, inadequate to the idea of loss and death. Grace was more incongruous than amazing. In Australia, the general pattern of leave-takings was rendered ludicrous by the inability of opera singers to actually get off the stage, guests to actually get into their car, or P&O liners to work up enough head of steam to break the fluttering coloured streamers. People simply could not bring themselves to say goodbye and act upon it – and so Melba's chorus would go around again and again. On the evidence, these last farewells, the funerary ones at least, gave rise to the bizarre, not to the pretentious absurdity of the European philosophers.

Our lives did not prepare us for death. Why, under this large canopy of ingenuous blue, at this remote distance from self-important events, why should we think upon it? Even the stark skeletons of ring-barked trees in the northern plains, or the grey ruins of flooded gums along some stretches of the Murray, killed off by what should have sustained them, seemed to confirm not loss, or decay, or recklessness, but persistence; they were strange markers of the enduring. They were still as tough as ever they were, and galahs would perch on them as happily as in a tree with a canopy of leaves.

Old Dave Parsons, the man from next door, was one such impressive gnarled monument to himself. He endeared himself to us as much by his eccentricities as by his excellent judgement in Christmas presents – boxing gloves, belts with ammunition pouches, the things you don't readily find in a quiet and untroubled neighbourhood. His shed held all sorts of treasures, a diesel motor that drove a series of slapping, jumping pulley belts, buckets of bolts and washers and bits of chain, axes, mallets, knives. You could play at any kind of villainy with such props. He had not one but two .303 rifles, which we once buried in his front lawn so that the Japanese wouldn't find them. His wife, without any humour at all, called him Dad. Esau-like, he was a hairy man, a whiskery man; his face was sandpaper. His cat had wire-brush fur. They shared a cup of scalding and very black tea on Sunday mornings: Parsons would pour out a saucer full while the cat rasped against the leg of his chair, and then – the bit we loved to watch – he put the cup down on the floor and slurped his own tea out of the saucer, because it was a more manageable temperature. The cat seemed to have lost all sensation of hot or cold over the years.

Parsons died some time after we shifted to the new house, and my mother was determined to make a personal gesture.

She would make a wreath from flowers in her own garden. Now, wreath-making is more difficult than it first appears, but it wasn't going to dismay my mother. She got some chicken wire and some straw and made something about the size of a small tyre, and she stuffed flowers into that. And it really looked quite creditable. The dismay was mine. I had to ride my bike with this arrangement, modestly covered by a number of overlapping half-opened paper bags, on my handlebars. It felt for a while vaguely Mediterranean, a goad for a big black bull. But more of an anxiety to me was the light rain which started to fall, and the thin brown paper got wet and started to disintegrate, apt emblem for the ceremony it was meant to grace; and then the flowers got wet and some started to loosen their contribution to the total effect as I pedalled faster and faster to get the sooner to my destination, a bedraggled impersonation of the grim rider.

The lying-in was at the married daughter's place; she took my mother's offering and I suppose it got put in the hearse with all the other professional floral tributes. But before that I was invited to take a last look at Parsons; and the shock to me was that the whiskers on his cheeks had kept on growing just as vigorously as always. In this case the Dad and Dave travesty was underscored at his funeral service by a conundrum lurking in the words of the hymn 'Immortal, invisible', in the affirmation that 'naught changeth thee'. For it was true in his case that nothing had changed him, or changed in him; and yet it was the very sign of on-going growth, his refusal to be utterly dead, that seemed so shocking, not so much a defiance of the natural law as an unawareness of its authority. He was still as always eccentric, outside the envelope as we might say these days (though the phrase is somewhat macabre in this instance). He was still giving splendid presents, presents of a kind to shock my mother. He had let me closer to the actuality of death than I had ever been before, because he demonstrated how closely interconnected with the living it was. And yet, though he was dear to us he was still the man from next door. There may have been a gap in the fence between us, but a fence there nevertheless was. His dying touched but did not touch me.

It was altogether a different matter the next time, with a much nearer encounter, and I was certainly not prepared for that when it came. My other grandfather, my maternal grandfather died, and I was interstate, at a distance; yet he was the one I felt close to. I had not been witness to his decline. He had continued to live in my mind in the big empty house at the beach front, just as always whenever I was allowed to stay there in those earlier times, a house full of echoes and chimes and stillness and salt air, glassed off from the persistent hush of the waves just across the esplanade. He used to let one half of the house during the summer months, but otherwise it stayed locked off, and we were aware of the vacancy, the hollowness, along the other side of the central passage. The original kitchen had been over on that side of the house, and beneath its linoleum were steps leading down to a cellar with dark water lapping across its floor. For the house had been built long ago on the crest of the leading sand-dune, and just behind that, as the Aborigines knew but not the new colonists apparently, was an accumulation of fresh water. The cellar was closed over permanently, but it was still there, a mysterious water cave with its own half-remembered reverberations. There were corrugated rainwater tanks out by the laundry, and my grandfather checked the water level in those every time he went past, rapping the ridges with his knuckles until the ringing resonance I loved to hear came to a flat rap, a sound which he, from his early years on the land, loved to hear.

The house itself re-echoed with the regular tock and quarter-hour chimes of the mantel clock, a fascination in itself as my grandfather could not get it level: he chocked up one leg with a two-shilling piece, and then another and so on around the four corners of the little temporal world so that the whole was mounted on separate stacks of coins. Half way along the central passage-way, standing on a column adult high and always cool to the touch, was a massive alabaster ice cavern, a hollowed iceberg perhaps, with polar bears poised on ledges; we were more intrigued by the cavern than the bears. In the front room, the sun room, which looked out through casement windows over the esplanade and out to spectacular sunsets across the Gulf, was a model sailing ship, anchored to a wall and sailing nowhere, certainly not over seas forlorn, a cross between the *Golden Hind* and the *Endeavour*. It had cannon spiked out of hatches along its sides, and a wheel that didn't swivel the rudder, and faded pennons.

This was a house I wandered happily through, without much coming across either of my grandparents. They were always doing something else somewhere else. The chances are that Nanna was out the front, beating on the side of an enamel billy full of scraps of everything, calling in the silver gulls. My grandfather could have been doing anything, up painting the roof or oiling the doorlocks of his car or sorting nails and screws in the shed. He had a curious and distinctive timbre to his voice. He seemed to carry echoes within him, perhaps the Devon echoes of his own grand-father. I would think of him when we read 'Drake's Drum' at school, and find his face behind Drake's pointy beard and airforce moustaches. The comparison was absurd of course, because my grandfather was all pink skinned and gleaming, with just a faint web of wispy white hair above his ears. But he could glare and stare down anybody even though he was a short man, and all but snort fire. He would have put the wind up the Spaniards. 'My godfather,' he'd say, and breathe heavily, and hold up his forefinger like a scolding school-teacher or a premier without a policy, and you knew that was the starting point for some forcefully expressed opinion – usually about some recent political ineptitude. He had stood for Parliament once, unsuccessfully, and none of those who got themselves elected thereafter could meet his expectations of them. State politics that is; the only sort that mattered. He lived by the forcefulness of his convictions; you did not readily contradict him, though sometimes to get him really going you might provoke him for a round or two.

When he was in his coffin, it was that beaky nose that was so prominent, the nostrils no longer flaring. The sight of him there was like a blow, a thwack that felt as though it had taken the living daylights out of me. My grandfather was in a different kind of hollow box now, one that held its resonances to itself, unlike the carrying echoes of his uneven mantel clock, and the shadow of another basement with its mysterious water lurked like an undertone. He had been undermined by other shifting sands, the fine white grains that searched out ways to trickle into his rock-solid house, to sift from one chamber to the other. How could we convince ourselves that conviction could sustain us now? 'We blossom and flourish as leaves on the tree/ And wither and perish ...' said the doleful hymn. Yet that isn't how it happened, or certainly not to us. Leaves dropped off, mostly from a kind of inattentiveness it seemed, or for no reason at all. Withering and perishing had nothing to do with us, though we had constantly before us the long-standing remnants of some other passing blight.

What we learned from all this was, I think, resistance. Awareness is of course cumulative. That is the principle underlying rote learning, the rather pleasant if mindless chanting of the seven times table. But there comes another different awareness, waiting like the heart's shadow at the schoolyard gate, premonitory, dread. We do not always know what to do with this. Somehow we learn not to be overwhelmed; meaning, as a defensive strategy, not to attach too much importance to matters like self-valuation. Back then we learned that death is not so much an absurdity – we did not aspire to such French profundities – as it is bizarre in its ceremonies. Death drew attention to itself as a disjunction. Whenever and however it happened, we were not prepared for it. Our lives had not prepared us for it. Why should it? But conversely, it did not seem ready for us.

The truth is we do not learn from the established past. If we did, we would already know from Voltaire that death is an absurdity, or from Nietzsche that it is about the loss of an older way of being, and the demise is ours. On the whole our learning tends to be empirical – certainly that was the case back then. We learn only, if at all, from the test of our own past. And it is another absurdity how often we fail that test. The young these days are called street-smart, meaning that they have an altogether updated, maybe newfangled, range of experiences which have formed them. The range of experiences I am re-visiting in these essays constitutes a different formative set, a different order, and presumably developed us in ways that were not street-smart. It is the characteristic range, the set, that interests me, not our perceived failures, eccentricities, or nonconformity in character building.

6

Of Our Own Making

When the disingenuous decade, the sixties, eventually arrived, it was all about persuading us of the unimportance of our dreary suburban lives. In the desert boots of existential despair we shuffled off to more wretched sloughs, as the hidden persuaders revealed to us their self-evident truths. We did live in ticky-tacky little boxes all in a row, and who could gainsay that? Theirs were words and sentiments we could understand, only too credible because familiar. And our own national prophets, Patrick White, Barry Humphries and the like, confirmed the worst about us. The curious consequence however was unexpected: by being predictable and just like everybody else, we had in fact extended ourselves, attached ourselves to the bigger picture; we were growing up.

The groundwork for all this, the trenches and formwork and reinforcing, was put in place a bit earlier, throughout the time of national reconstruction. We knew about the national effort from the Movietone News; but we went on pretty much as we always had. Business as usual, mainly small business. Minding our own business. And yet for all the fifties' hat and gloves ceremonial of going to town, and other imperatives like six o'clock closing and Sunday visiting, suburban life was not just an opaque banality. Something was always happening, there was always something to look at. The council workers might be about, in stained hats and dry leather boots and shiny-backed waistcoats, poisoning weeds along the galvanised iron fences, or around the creosote boles of telegraph poles – that is, what thistles and dock was left after the baker's horse had given up picking there. Mechanisation had not completely routed an older order. Stobie poles had not yet blighted all the sidestreets and bread delivered by horse and cart was somehow healthier, more honest. It sometimes had little bits of string in it. Up and down the street, early in the summer mornings, men in brown dressing-gowns, striped pyjamas and carpet slippers, and with the just-delivered newspaper under their arm, would vie for the small piles of droppings left by the milkman's horse. Good for the roses.

In summer, gangs from the Department of Agriculture would come storming into the backyards of suburbia, to strip all the fruit from the fruit-trees: another outbreak of fruit-fly had just been reported. Inevitably, one of the chooks would go broody, and hatch out a clutch of chickens. Even more inevitably, one of the cats would have kittens. We probably knew as much about that sort of thing as any farm children. We weren't at such a disadvantage.

There were skills to acquire, mastering marbles, raising silkworms, flipping yo-yos. In the intervals between the displacement of one fad by another we monitored the exchange rate for swapping comics, stamps, bubble-gum cards. Some sort of trade was always going on. There were the usual events of the calendar – the Show, with its sample bags and sideshows and Cowley's pie-cart and shitty cattle, and Guy Fawkes Day with its crackers and bonfires and potatoes baked in the ashes. There were seasonal events like blackberrying in the Hills, and mushrooming in the pad-docks near the foothills, and shelling almonds to earn pocket money for Christmas. And there were more infrequent occa-sional events like Royal Visits and Billy Graham crusades and Facts of Life films for fathers and sons in the Town Hall: my grandfather escorted us, and was no less amazed than we were to see spermatozoa huge as sea-lions frisking around on the screen. I have to suppose that my father knew what he was about. We never told him what he missed.

All sorts of things you could do and see in the suburban round of days. Scale one fence and you could have an egg-fight with over-ripe bantam eggs in the long grass behind the grocer's shop. Over another, behind the motor-bike shop where Jack Young's tarnishing World Championship belt, as big as a corset, lay among dusty chains and cogs in the window, you could find a couple of flea-bitten kangaroos and a sulky emu in a chook-wire run. Advance Australia. Over another to sneak the only mulberry leaves in the neigh-bourhood for your silkworms. And to really test your nerve, you could run through the grounds of the Catholic Church and hope you wouldn't be turned into a goat by an outraged priest. But you didn't want to push your luck too often.

And there were any number of occasions for initiations, investitures, enrolments, experiences of that kind. We were encouraged to be joiners: we joined everything. We became members of the Ovaltinies and a certificate and bronze lapel badge arrived in the post – we wouldn't learn to say mail for a good many years yet. America was still pretty much confined to Donald Duck, soft drinks and bubble-gum. We thought about joining the Argonauts and all the other clubs sponsored by radio programs – which we thought of as broadcasts on the wireless. We copied out jokes and sent them in to Possum's Page in the *Sunday Mail*, where every week someone called Nyorie Bungye creamed off all the different coloured certificates for her endless stream of original contributions, stories and poems and drawings, and we all grew to resent her. We didn't believe in her, even though, or just because, there she was Sunday after Sunday. At some stage we went to the Church of Christ hall after school, lured by the temperance equivalent of cakes and ale, and there we endured for too long a shiny-domed man with a whole calendar of illustrative material. 'Here is a cow: cows drink water. Here is a dog: dogs drink water. Here is ...' he droned on endlessly, and without any enthusiasm, while he turned over yet another picture and we wriggled on the hard little wooden chairs. He had mistaken his audience. 'And here is a man; but oh dear, no, man does not only drink water.' The raspberry cordial tried to make amends. And somewhere in all that we appeared to have signed the pledge. Well, it was another certificate.

On occasion, joining actually required something of us – joining the Cubs, for instance. In front of a circle of those already initiated, intent and unnervingly quiet except for here and there an occasional dry cough brought on by dust percolating down from the rafters, and in the half-light thrown out by one partly covered bulb, you tried to master self-consciousness and repeat the words of your pledge. Long still shadows converged at your feet; the sense of having to meet some unstated expectation was, though briefly, intensely felt. 'On my honour, I promise ...' It was a serious reflection, at a young age, to discover not only that you had a code of honour but that it could be binding. One hand trembled on the furled flag, the other made an equally unconfident salute. Moths clattered about the single point of light. And then came the release, and the return of disbelief, as the Cubs did their not very good imitation of wolves, hunkering down and, as everybody knows, shouting dib-dib-dib, Akela-we-will-do-our-best, and whooping and howling out into the street, out into the night where the mysteries really belonged and other crazed shadows and flitting moths. And the stirred-up dust began to settle all over again.

There wasn't anything really special about that. Anyone could be a Cub or Brownie, or later a Scout or Girl Guide. Everyone was. All you had to remember was how to tie a reef knot. Left over right and right over left. Baden-Powell's contribution to the Empire rested on this vision of millions of children intent on tying reef knots. Give me a rope long enough and two free ends and I will restrain the world. Sometimes it actually did prove useful, as when you needed to add another colour of wool to your tomboy-stitch.

Likewise, though it felt unfamiliar for a bit, there wasn't anything really special about going up from primary school to high school. Or later, sitting for public exams in the Exhibition Hall at the Showgrounds. Because visibly, everyone else was doing it too. We joined youth groups, we played team sports. There was any amount of group activity in the suburban almanac. What the suburbs did not seem to promote was an opportunity for that more important experience of confrontation with the self, more properly a *rite de passage* than an initiation, in that there could be very little preparation for it.

The bigger rites we took in our stride, perhaps because they were out of proportion for us, too big, and remote. The fatalities of the war had taken place a long way away, a long way back; we were wartime babies, too young to remember any of that. For some years our grandmother had complained about her swollen ankles, and she was too puffed to dance about as Father Christmas any more. She seemed to recede behind her glasses; she turned yellow

and took to her bed. We paid dutiful visits on Sunday afternoons, but we quickly tired of standing in the poorly lit
bedroom – even the light through the blinds was yellow like
decay – and the sickly smell of her cancer drove us out to
play with the old bleary-eyed, nicotine-coloured collie, or
to look at the bantams in amongst a clump of bamboo down
at the end of the yard. Not an unclaimed egg in sight.
Grandma was buried, as she had feared, in a rainstorm and
we didn't have to go, so for us the euphemism was the truth.
She passed away.

Even National Service, when the time came, failed my
generation. In spite of the excited talk of bristling retired
majors, this was not a means of making men of us, whatever
good it might have done for Australia. National Service
provided trucks and manpower for fighting floods and
bushfires; it provided a conscripted defence force against
the country itself. But it didn't really allow us to know our
enemy, nor to know ourselves. For one thing, it was by that
time a lottery, and easily avoided. It paid no heed to the
individuality of the servicemen (equality of opportunity
hadn't happened then) and indeed seemed designed, as all
things military, to stamp out any such notion. The self was
to be submerged in the greater glory of the platoon, regi-
ment, whatever – the team. The one great disaster would be
for the individual soldier to think for himself, and of himself.
Not that there is any possible originality in this reflection;
it has ever been thus. But in terms of actually helping people
to grow up, the government couldn't arrange that. That
is something you do on your own. And at the time I am
remembering, the best chance for it still lay in the country.

The point was not the country itself, but that it was
away from home. In Adelaide as in the other cities, the
custom had evolved that at a certain stage it was appropriate

to get a summer job somewhere in the country. We did not say up the country – that was the quaint idiom of romantic novelists. For an earlier generation, a summer job had meant spending weeks out in the blazing sun, out in the paddocks sewing up wheat-bags, a job that teachers (Hal Porter among them) seemed to have pretty well organised for themselves. Bulk handling began to put an end to it. But you could always get a job picking fruit. Fruit-picking was dead easy. All you needed was a pair of boots, a pair of shorts, and a hat. That was all there was to it: you just walked up a ladder and put out your hand and picked. You didn't even need to know how to tie a reef knot.

The one worry was about the hat. Hats had to look right: you couldn't fake age and experience into a hat, and yet you didn't want to give away your novice status with brand new headgear obviously just separated from its price-tag. Much of the journey up from Adelaide was spent in carefully crushing the original shape out of it, without collapsing the thing into a droopy bonnet. A second anxiety was about wearing any hat at all, because hats for men were definitely unfashionable around the city. Only old blokes and country people wore hats, and commercial travellers – people who lived inside their own time-frame and didn't notice that the times, at least as determined in the city, were a-changing. The story was that if you saw someone driving along and wearing a hat, you took extra care – for it would be one of those three, and they were likely to do any unpredictable thing. Or maybe it could be a policeman; whichever, you learned to be on your guard about hats.

Fruit-blocks weren't about fashion, but they were about image, just as at all work sites in this nominally careless and cheerfully unconcerned country. There's a subtlety in the signals that are given. Your boots might be too clean, your socks too fussily pulled up; you might be too polite or too much at ease with the boss; you might even be guilty of working too hard. You have to learn above all how to fit in, how to go along with the others, how not to be different. It's not egalitarianism, it's not mateship that governs this country, but anxiety about being different.

And the men had their ways of making you welcome.

So it was that, late one afternoon, with strong shadows raddled over the hot red sand at the end of a row of peaches, and lean pullets, scrawny black orpingtons with indecently exposed chests, just beginning to emerge from under the skirts of the grapefruit trees, the boss handed you over to the foreman. He would show you what you would be doing the next morning. There was the ritual exchange of g'day, a bit difficult across the rattle and shake of an enormous old tractor–he had just finished dragging the cultivator down between the rows.

Good lookin' hat you got there. But y' haven't got the bash right. Here, give us it fer a bit. Know anything about peaches? This is a good peach: here, stick it in yer hat, have it fer tea. An' this is a really good nectarine ... apricots ... grapes over there. Got yerself a fruit salad, hey.

And quicker than you would ever see him move again, he had the whole lot down on the sand in front of the idling tractor and rolled the tarnished juggernaut right over it. So you spent the next half hour scrubbing out your hat in the irrigation channel; and that is how it acquired an authentic shapelessness and bucolic discoloration, just like everyone else's.

On the first morning, as with many mornings, at an impossibly early hour and with the light strangely clear, the pickers threaded their way through the trees to where the tractor had tugged the trailer. The boss was already there, with a huge flask of shockingly strong black bitter tea, and a great stack of soggy toast and Vegemite. Somehow it made you respect the likely heat of the day to come.

His mistake wasn't the hapless tea and toast. His mistake was that he brought it out himself every morning, so that it wasn't a mark of thoughtfulness and appreciated, it was expected, and on the way to becoming an entitlement. He tried to be hearty, as though he could break down the necessary division between him and his employees; but he was a small wiry man and it didn't fit. He would be first up the ladders of course, and he'd tear into the apricots, grabbing handsful of leaves and snapping twigs, and behind his back we would point out that he was picking too green. We didn't want him to be one of us. We had more respect for the job we were doing. We probably had more respect for the trees. But most importantly, he hadn't earned the right to be one of the pickers. Not that anyone was likely to fill his hat with fruit and run over it with the tractor. The point was that the boss didn't stay with the job. He just didn't put in a whole day. He was always off starting some other thing around the block, and then needing the foreman to come and do it properly; or he was off to meetings in the local town, because he was very active on the District Council.

So we would have the benefit of his company and his example for the first part of the morning. Two or three pickers would be on a tree at a time. Nobody worked on the same tree as the boss. Which meant that as the morning went on he would gradually be left behind, little bit by bit. No matter how he tore and stripped, it just wasn't possible for him to keep up. You would look down a row and see his skinny pallid legs at the top of a ladder while the rest of him disappeared into a tree, and someone would move the trailer on so that he always had to carry his bucket a little further. We were quietly resisting subordination and coercion, though we never talked about it. We had contracted to work, not to be bossed around.

These little manoeuvres added to the sweetness of the day. 'Reckons he can pick and prune at the same time,' the foreman would laugh quietly across his shoulder, rolling his eyes at the scurf of green that always identified the boss's buckets. And by mid-morning, the boss would walk up to us, and an intent silence would fall while he watched. We didn't know which of us he had his eye on; we were absolutely concentrated on apricots, and we didn't need any hint about picking the fruit a bit greener ourselves. He had blazing blue eyes and exploding bushy eyebrows, and his face was ready to catch fire – he was one of those blue-lipped red-heads. He had a smile like he'd read about it one time. His hair was tight and crinkly, and the same colour as the sand he scuffed up with his boots – the sand caught in the pale hairs of his livid shins. He liked to wear a kind of faded army rig – shorts and boots and stained slouch hat. He would stand there snorting down his fiery nostrils, and you knew his crazy ginger eyebrows would be wriggling around, and he would find something to criticise. He had to, before he could go.

When he had gone the day really started. You could feel a rhythm develop in your work, like a long stilted dance around the trees. They were mainly happy mindless days, the pickers slowly working up and down the rows, filling buckets and emptying them again. There was a steady patter of chiacking, apparently harmless but able to turn malicious given half a chance. Long sardonic yarns drifted through the branches. Soon they would drop to murmurs; distant sounds failed to intrude in this leafy domain, and only the scrape of ladders, the muffled footfalls in the loose sandy furrows would be heard. And when the tractor rolled forward, immense and sun-rusted, the most bell-like plinking of cool waterfalls came from inside those huge tyres – they were part-filled with water to make it easier to keep up the air pressure.

It was quiet down among the trees, and good. You would be canopied inside your own imprecise and lazy thoughts, though what you were thinking it would be hard to say. Here you drifted into a sense of geniality, of *bon accord*, under your hat, under the trees, under the great empty whitish blue sky. Your eye absorbed the different colours in the apricots, the reds and whites and browns and blacks of the bark; you took in with your breath the metallic smells of ladders and buckets and sprinkler pipes, the sharp cidery smell of fermenting fruit; you heard but did not notice the remote sounds of trucks and windmills and pumps and an occasional crow. And your mind did nothing with all this. You were beginning to merge with some other place than your own.

Beyond the shelter of the trees, the heat beating up from the earth struck at your legs, your elbows, your cheeks – a hat couldn't protect you from everything, even one worn inside out. It was as though the heat in the air held down the radiant surface heat, locked with it and would not let it escape. Out here the baking sand had not been turned over so carefully. Wicked three-cornered jacks lay strewn around like shrapnel from exploded landmines. Weeds – this-tles, mallow, dock – and clumps of paspalum all along the irrigation channels lent a pungency to the air, and a thin grey yabby-ish smell hovered over the trickling water. Out here the vines were bulging, waiting for us to finish clean-picking the stone fruit, waiting for the itinerant Italian grape-pickers. The Italians didn't wear hats: the women wore scarves and the men wore knotted handkerchiefs. And like the vines, they all bulged, in all sorts of unsightly places. That was hard work, out in the vines, hoicking up bucket after bucket of grapes, stacking them on the trailer, taking them over to the dipping tank and then spreading the bunches on the drying racks. It was all stoop and twist and lift, back-wrenching stuff.

In the cutting shed was another kind of heat, which weighed down like an imminent headache. It made you irritable to be in there, slashing the fruit with a knife curved like a butcherbird's bill, setting it out on crinkled cardboard sheets, especially the stinking mushy apricots for 'slabs'. After a while a kind of sludge would build up between your fingers and on the palms of your hands, your wrists. Relations were uneasy in there. This was the women's domain, the boss's wife, the foreman's wife, girls from nearby fruit-blocks, a couple of casuals, and we weren't at all sure of our place when we were told to help in the shed – if say the water allocation had come through and the fruit was still wet from the sprinklers. It wasn't our place, and we didn't have a place to fit into. You suspected a hierarchy, a pecking order, you could feel it but you couldn't see it. Conversations always took on a more self-conscious edge; and there had to be conversation. You couldn't just drift off in such fixed and constraining proximity. There was a lot of expressive sniffing too. Sound was different in there, under the dinged corrugated iron and sagging home-welded trusses. It was a relief to take the milky grey cardboard trays out to the rough and ready drying racks, slapdash and unfinished, tensioned with any old lump of wood that had been handy at the time; a relief to straighten your drooping shoulders, breathe the pungent smell of the pears already spread out, acrid with sulphur; and a relief to hear the women's talk start up again, back in the shed. Outside, you knew your place. Back there, well you weren't there long enough to find out where or what it was.

And when, as it had to in that country, the heat got too much, but the picking and dipping and cutting and drying had gone well, there just might be a lift to the river. The river. It didn't need to be named. A very slight weighting on the definite article made clear to everyone just what you meant. The river. It was – it is – the state's lifeline, literally as well as metaphorically. That was our drinking water the Easterners were pissing into upstream, or throwing fishguts into. The river was symbolically important too, the one place where we could claim an equal footing with the eastern states. Our river was as big as their river. Bigger, probably. But then niggling doubt sets in – probably more placid. Not as heavily treed. Their dark stands of rivergum further up give way lower down to a thin line right along our verge. Behind that fringe of leaves are the fruit-blocks, extending as far back as the irrigation pumps could maintain enough pressure. And wherever the land rises a little, then the low cliffs are limestone and clay, and hot as a baking oven.

Here and there, at places the locals knew about, at the end of tracks through paddocks and sagging fences and bent gates patched for no good reason with rabbit-proof wire, were small stretches of river sand, with a big rivergum or two for shade, and some bulrushes upstream to show that a bit of a sandbank jutted out a way – an ideal spot for a swim and a picnic tea. People had been coming to places like these for years, possibly thousands of years. Charred twigs and sticks, the residue of numberless campfires, discoloured the sand and flecked it with bits of black. A few logs lay about, ancient and woolly grey, too heavy to shift, too heavy to burn. And out past the calm of the backwater, past the eddies, the big curdy river bore on down, muddy coloured like most great rivers, a great steady surge, powerful rather than fast, but quick enough too if you kept your eye on a branch of willow twisting and rolling out in the main current. You had to respect a river that big, as big as they come in this country.

This is about finding out afterwards something you didn't know before. It's called growing up, and nobody can tell you about it, you just find out for yourself. It's about arriving at some kind of estimation of your abilities, and liabilities, some kind of realistic self-appraisal. All too often, about how foolish you can be, how dangerously close to disaster you can come without thinking. It's a different matter to take on the thrill of anticipated danger, pushing the edge of a capacity you know you have. But for someone who couldn't – still can't – swim all that well, to do what all the young blokes did, swim the river, that was just plain stupid. Nobody set up the challenge, or called my bluff; I'd just heard the others talking about how and when they did it, skiting under the fruit trees, and this seemed an opportunity. Nobody to impress but myself; the others were comfortable with their picnic. Besides, they'd seen other young fellows swim the river from time to time, and how were they to know I might not be in the same league.

League seems apt. At this place the river sweeps around in a great bend; it is wider than at other places, by local gossip a mile across. I'd doubt that now, but that was the kind of distance I was imagining, and for someone who puffed to do a length of the City Baths, I can't imagine what I was imagining. Sheer madness. It didn't start out like that. 'Going for a bit of a swim,' I called out, and waded in. Bit of breast-stroke to start with, in case they recognised I had no style with the Australian crawl; so at that stage I was trying to impress somebody other than myself. And it was fairly easy going in the quiet water. Even enjoyable – you had time to notice the afternoon sun turning the low bank on the other side a burnished gold, you could hear crows and galahs – crows were more my pace – somewhere upstream, and a diesel pump burbling away in amongst a scraggy stand of bulrushes. And a waterhen scooting about. Steadily I was working my way out into what you might call real water, taking my time. I was in no hurry; besides, when I turned and looked back to the riverbank, nobody was taking any notice. If anyone had to be convinced that this was just going to be simply a matter of doing it, it was me.

I wasn't completely stupid. I had worked out that I would have to swim upstream into the current, though I had no idea how much allowance to make for that; so I was sort of ready for something, but nowhere near ready for it when the surge hit. I could easily enough have turned around at that stage, and come on back in. Only I didn't. The way I figured it, there's no great skill required in swimming, a bit like fruit-picking really, or tying knots. You just keeping kicking and moving your arms around, just keep on doing it. That's all there is to it. Except out there, in the middle, the water won't leave you alone. It comes at you and keeps coming at you, it pushes over one shoulder all the time, and it isn't a constant surface, it keeps breaking over your face just as you are breathing, sucking in air, gasping. And once you start coughing you lose your momentum and whatever rhythm you had invented, and then you start to feel the current sweeping you away. And that's when you panic. That's when you begin to know what you are in for. Right out there in the middle, even a bit further perhaps.

Go for it, Macbeth. Right, Macduff.

Twice before I'd nearly drowned. The first time was at a swimming pool in the Gorge, next to some tea-rooms. It must have been a weekend in the summer – the place was jam-packed, and I'd bet not much chlorinated either. The pool was decidedly unprofessional, rendered with polished cement, and slippery if not slimy. I was maybe five or six, dog-paddling about close enough to the edge, but not an edge that was any use to me once I got out of my depth. Each time I reached for it my hand slipped right off and under I went, again and again and again. Each time I went down I could see all those livid forms, legs and trunks and arms wavering about, and lots of silvery bubbles in the lemonade-coloured water, and hear the bell-shaped silence of all that weird and dislocated activity; and then I'd gasp up through the surface and all the noise would burst in, shouting and squealing and splashing, and then lunge and grasp and slip again, back down under the water, each time deeper, each time more fascinated by the fact that water has skeins of shadows inside itself, rippling and dancing, fascinated to be secretly down here in a deepening shadow, nobody knowing I was looking up from such a depth, and those receding bubbles up there, they had ceased to have anything to do with me – and some strong hand grabbed my shoulder and hefted me up and right out of the pool, on to the warm cement surround, but not warm enough to stop me shaking and shivering for a very long time.

Later I reasoned from that, and from the safety of body-surfing (well, this is Adelaide surf we are talking about), that it was somehow more secure to swim underwater than to try to keep above it, as though that forestalled sinking; which is how I ran into trouble the second time. On one of those really hot summer nights when there was no relief at all even long after the sun had finally set, the family drove down to the beach along with at least half the entire population of the city, and out there in the dark I was doing my torpedo stunt, quite minding my own business – when suddenly I was in the middle of massive wrestling and groping and threshing, my head being roughly fumbled, something pushing me down into the sand, pinning me down under water. Blackness, and memory says I could hear? feel? the thumping of feet shifting about on the sea-bed, though maybe it was the pounding in my ears. I suppose my panic was nothing compared with that of the man whose legs I'd swum into, who didn't know what was about to bite him in halves and wasn't about to think calmly about it; no philosopher, his panic turned into anger rather than relief when I managed to roll clear and surface. I was out of there fast, disappearing into a safer darkness.

And here we are, I was thinking, about to go down for the third time. Too many different things to think about all at once – how far forwards and how far back complicated by the sideways sweep, the water surface no longer sliding but breaking up into small choppy waves, ripping along. Volume, and colour, and force and mass – here close up was what it had looked like the time we went to see the floods at Mannum. You expect water to be translucent; this was murky, opaque, thick with colour, somehow solid. And that other dimension you'd refused to let yourself think about, below; all of whatever was down there, deeper and deeper layers of every-thing unthinkable, unfathomable and unimaginable, things – what things? – that were down in that darkness, and not rum-bling, but avid, intent, dangerous. You wanted to be able to touch bottom, and you were terrified of the prospect of touching anything, worse, of being touched. And if you slipped below the surface, no, you had to keep up to the light, and glubbing gets you nowhere. No time for superstition, no time to remember the drowning sheep I'd tried to rescue one year just off the bank, just a rush of blind, frantic terror because this was all a lot bigger than I was, bigger than the surge that had carried me away from my parents in the crowd cheering the end of the war, bigger than anything I had ever known, and maybe bigger than I could ever know. Now I really knew what it meant to be out of my depth. And me all alone.

It's a tired cliché to write 'tired cliché', and another to write of burning and bursting lungs; but what's a cliché for unless to remind us that others have been there before? Such shaping experiences are new to each of us at the time, and none the less important for that. The point is that you don't have to be exceptional to encounter them. So yes, my throat was rasping by the time I'd found my way into smoother waters, by the time I'd cautiously felt about with one foot, and found the disgusting soft unresisting muddy bottom with whatever it covered underneath that – the sedimentary history of the district if I'd been collected enough to think of it. Its only significance at that moment was sensational – of the gelid and rotting and formless. I was beyond thinking. Any energy I had was directed to lurching towards the shore, trembling and weakened and feeling as if some weight were pulling me down, as if something still wasn't prepared to let me go. Staggering through the last hard yards of weed to the gentle proof of lapping waters.

Where was the triumph, the sense of achievement in that? There was none. For the immediate problem I faced, once I'd recovered my breath and some little poise, was how to get back. The drama was, I could sense it, about to be re-played; and a tentative push back into the river was enough to let me know that there was no way I could make it back on my own. None of the blokes had talked about this part of the challenge. I looked about on the riverbank and found a log which I thought might enable me to paddle back – but as soon as I'd pushed it out as far as the depth would let me, the current seized it, twisted and rolled it, and despairingly I watched it race away. There had been nothing like enough buoyancy in it to help me anyway: a curious expression that, water-logged. And just a few strokes of my own out towards the mainstream was enough to convince me again of what I knew.

There was nothing else for it. I had taken my measure and found it inadequate. Back on the bank, I whistled and waved my arms and even shouted 'hoy!' – that must have come from some book or other. Nobody says 'hoy'. And all that waving and whistling felt back to front, a kind of parody of celebration. Eventually I was noticed; and after some long time, for they'd had to go looking, a little boat put out from among the reeds. The rowing was ragged and untidy, and left me plenty of time to reflect on what I might have to say for myself once it had zig-zagged across the river – they hadn't allowed sufficiently for the pace of the current, and the late afternoon breeze picking up and seeming to increase its force. There wasn't in fact much that needed to be said. Shaded by his faded and floppy hat, the boss allowed himself a brief private smile; and bent to his oars, and all the sound was his heavily nasal breathing and the clunk of the rowlocks lifting and dropping back into the gunwale, and the strange quavering mockery of that distant crow.

All the long row back across the river nothing was said, and I sat huddled inside my own unhappiness, and the collapse of whatever conceit of myself I'd had to start out with. It had not yet occurred to me that there had been some little maturity of another kind in calling for help; nor that that should also be the real absurdity. We all find our own moments of truth, and as with the ancient mysteries, witnesses are not necessary. It is our own experience that supplies the essential knowledge; what seems to count is whether we are at the stage of readiness to learn from it. More interesting perhaps is that the moment finds us, when we are ready – and when the first stage is to learn that we are not as ready as we imagine. Once started on this process, there is in fact no turning back. And finally, a significant part of what we learn is our essential loneliness. The process of separation of the self from the communal is evidently both necessary and inevitable. It is also, as each of us learns, painful. We are diminished at the same moment we begin to grow, and discover our minority just as we are reaching for our majority.

The season was over for me. There wasn't anything else I was about to learn. Besides, other rites were summoning, the recommencement of the student's year, coming of age birthday parties ... It was time to head back to the city. I could get a ride back with a local truckie who was taking a load down to the markets – second grade fruit. The best went to Melbourne. Second rate was reckoned good enough for Adelaide. The deal was that I had to help load the truck – late in the day, after the fruit or maybe the day itself had cooled off. Either way, it was a slog after a whole day of picking, then packing. A cold beer at the end of it was a welcome gesture – my first beer, offered as from one worker to another. Here I was leaving, and I had just arrived. I put my hat down, wiped my forehead, threw my gear in the back of the cab, and we were off, on the long slow haul down from the riverland, leaving behind the soft pink dusty roads with their crushed limestone verges, leaving behind the fast fading sunset – leaving behind my hat – and through the hills, staring ahead into the darkness, looking for something to say, looking out into another darkness that had opened out beneath me for long enough to let me know that there was more than I would ever get to know, and perhaps more than I wanted to know. Yet in getting to know that much, we get to know something of ourselves. Such experiences aren't exclusive like the mysteries, but they are exclusive in that they are our own, and of our own making. So too, little by little we understand the place we live in, the place we make for ourselves in it.

7

The Working Man's Paradise

In South Australia, the most deeply felt conviction is that anything significant happens interstate. We have missed out on the national emblems and icons, and likewise the costumery of history belongs elsewhere. Australian natural history belongs to the eastern states, it seemed to have passed us by. With the local absence of recognisable iconography, national and cultural emblems are remote, extraneous, incidental, and possibly all the more revered for being so. The history we were taught – indeed, history pretty much as it is still taught – is a romantic narrative, literally make believe; whereas our own experiences, whether inherited or direct, were and are like our workaday shoes, familiar but not for dancing in. Curiously, it felt and still feels right that the emblems and the important stories belong elsewhere. The truly significant cultural details acquire their esteem by not being so readily accessible. They are treasured in the imagining, like Keats's nightingale and Wordsworth's daffodils; or like Shakespeare's folios in protective custody somewhere in America. We go on knowing they exist, and can make them our own as far as we want.

In Adelaide, green and gold is more likely to mean late winter soursobs than wattle blossom; the imagery needs to be rearranged, the actual colour of the landscape reviewed. Here, clouds of almond blossom are a passing fancy against the bald hills of the southern vales (thinking of these as a region, and as a rolling plain rather than as valleys); to be followed in due season, when the nuts have ripened and the leathery lips of the husks split and curl back, by hordes of galahs hanging on to the trees like so many shrieking Christmas decorations. The characteristic motif at the year's end is blue, a blue so bright it becomes crystalline, splendid on mornings that ting with the freshness of the very first of summer, and there's as yet no hint of dust in the crisp and sparkling air. The grass in the parklands has not yet browned off, the calls of piping shrikes drill across any open spaces, and all down the suburban streets roses in the front gardens vibrate with colour and perfume.

This is the making of summer. The dread heat of late January and February – and truth to tell, March too – is another season altogether, a season out of hell, so harrowing it is given no name, and blasted as any Old Testament furnace. But the summer that promises so well, that used unerringly to show its first early stirrings in the second week of the Royal Show, goes on to make its presence increasingly felt in dull headaches at the annual public and university examinations and slips the leash of holiday feelings, this is when you feel most strongly the intimations of new energy, of some important and imminent change.

At this time, all along the main roads the shopkeepers used to set out their wares with a renewed zest. The shopping strips, vaguely suggestive in an antipodean and localised provincial way of England's ubiquitous High Street, still constitute the thinnest remnant of a suburban village whose real life lies unremarked in the banal streets laddering off the spine of the main road. Business has a way of not noticing how unimportant it is; yet it cannot afford to doubt its own priority, even when it is patently not identified with a high pressure centre of commerce. And its logic is looped. If business doesn't impress itself, how can it persuade us? At the time I am telling of, the fifties and early sixties, you felt aggrieved if there was a queue in the bank, the Savings Bank of South Australia, which had given every schoolchild a tin money box in approximately the likeness of Head Office and with a lock in its base, and you could get the coins to slide out of the slot if you shook it slowly upside down and from side to side. You certainly did not wait long to be served in the shops; indeed, they were embarrassingly prompt in the chemist's, and couldn't wait to get you out on to the streets again. Everyone minded everyone else's business. And everyone noticed if ever you went into the police station.

At this time of year, when November eases into December, a change could be perceived. This was a time of anticipation. The signs were mainly tentative, the shopkeepers standing about, most of them in different kinds of aprons – the butcher in dark blue and white stripes, a half apron, and a hardened leather pouch on his hip with an array of long slender knives and a sharpening steel; the limping greengrocer in a full leather apron with a kind of marsupial pouch for his order book, the shoe repairer in a shinier and heavier leather apron, the hardware assistants in grubby cloth, the hairdresser in a white cotton jacket ... The different aprons and coats were quite unremarkable yet were almost as significant as the regalia of the ancient guilds. Everyone seemed to be waiting, waiting for something to happen, on the Micawber principle that something or someone was bound to turn up soon. In the mean time, they were disposed to enjoy the early morning sun.

So as with any marketplace in the world, they busied

themselves with setting out their wares, arranging and re-arranging and changing their displays, polishing the fruit for example, or moving the best produce forward and shifting buckets of cut flowers from one advantageous position to another. Or they would be standing outside their shops, wiping their hands on their aprons or calling out in a friendly chippy way to each other: mannerisms of either the Cockney or the archetypal vendor, intimately colloquial and comfort-able. They all knew each other well, and could be as insulting as they liked provided it was meant as camaraderie. The barber would be sweeping up yesterday's leavings across his linoleum floor, the butcher putting out trays of best mince – was there a worst mince? – from the cool-room in the inner recesses of his shop, or fresh sawdust around his big chopping block, and bumping the sides of hogget hanging by their hocks from grey metal hooks, or jostling huge skeins of fat sausages also hanging from the rack. At the grocer's (it was too English just to say 'grocery') they'd be opening up a great wheel of semi-matured cheese, or hanging up a fresh and slowly uncoiling fly-paper. Outside the shoe-shop they would be arranging a rack of slippers tied together at the heel by a loop of string, hardly the season for slippers you would think, but just the shot for Dad this Christmas.

At this time of year the greengrocers' shops were sud-denly mounded with colourful fresh fruit from up the river, great crates and pyramids of bright apricots and peaches and nectarines, and huge bunches of grapes that would have put Canaan out of sorts, and trays of fat dark red cherries from the Adelaide Hills; and in those days skeins of twisted coloured paper were hung in elegant long swooping loops from cornice to cornice, from light fixture to doorframe. Concertinaed paper Christmas bells dangled in the display windows. Exotic fruit like pomegranates would appear, and boxes of figs. Tasteful tinsel arrangements hung from the venetian blinds in the window of the ladies' hairdressing salon, a discreet establishment, though the songs wafting from the wireless in the reception area were starting to sound a tad perky. And outside all the shops the junior employees, delivery boys and counterhands would be sweeping the footpath, mainly cigarette butts and dead matches and tram tickets, and those on the western side of the road were rolling up the long canvas blinds that hung from the edge of the dingy iron awnings, and tying the pull cords to brackets on the verandah posts.

Everywhere you looked, people were busying themselves, or more accurately going through the motions of readying themselves for the season that had not yet begun, the day that had not yet started. Expectations ran, as every year at this time, ahead of likelihood; the customers were not yet customers. They were walking past the shops, stopping only to chat for a minute or two with the lady who ran the deli or someone cleaning the windows at the draper's. Their business was elsewhere, perhaps up the steps to the Postal and Telegraph Office with its entrance alcove of stamp machines and public notices about last year's taxation returns and Post Early for Christmas, and its big heavy swinging doors into the Post Office proper. All these signs showed the summer holidays were no longer just a promise, they were on their way. In the sidestreets, verandahs were being mopped, wooden doorsteps rubbed with shoe polish, driveways hosed off and under the carport alongside the garage, caravans were being swept out and washed down. Fences might get a lick of paint, front windows were certainly being vigorously cleaned. And to help clear the Christmas mail out of the way, the Post Office required conscientious and reliable lads who must have their own bicycles in a state of good repair.

All sorts of extra jobs were available at this time. Messenger boys were put on to deliver for the chemist, though why there should be an increased demand for toothpaste and cough syrup at the healthy end of the year remains unclear; in part, it seems, businesses put on extra temporary staff because other businesses were putting on extra staff. But the Post Office really did need additional hands to cope with all the Christmas cards and bills sent out before the end of the year. And the readily available pool were the students. The regular postmen were suspicious, and some were antagonistic. To them, advanced level education meant privilege; and it was certainly no guarantee of common nous. Self-interest was a part of this too: the more students that were put on, the less overtime for the posties.

How the application was made I do not now remember. This being the Post Office, of course there were forms to fill in. Adelaide being Adelaide, no doubt it helped that somebody knew somebody; or someone who had done it the previous year passed on advice about who you had to speak to and when. That was always the way of it – word of mouth and personal recommendation was the standard procedure, if not due process. Maybe that is inevitably the way of things in small towns and not overlarge cities, where if everybody doesn't actually know everybody else, they at least know some intermediary. You would be hard put to it to find six degrees of separation. In a small enough community nobody is at a disadvantage because everyone is in some measure known, or known about. Our contemporary pre-occupation with due process is the signature of an impersonal culture.

The day begins early in the Post Office, when the letters for the morning delivery are sorted, and the only other sign of activity in the sleepy, sunny streets is the milkman finishing off his round, or quite possibly the newspaper being delivered – the morning *Advertiser* tightly rolled and bent to a boomerang shape, and hurled from a not-so-slowly cruising Holden. On that first day, as the first day of anything – school, for example, or another country – everything is a novelty and a revelation, as though a new world is being opened up. The first sight of anything is always anomalous. You see more clearly than you ever will again, and yet you do not quite know what you are looking at. The detail does not make sense; being unpredictable, it is all absorbed and absorbing where later it is barely glanced at because it can be presumed. By the same token, it is recalled with greater difficulty because not remembered in that same dissociated way, for it is inevitably fitted into a pattern of meaning that becomes apparent subsequently.

What I recall without any uncertainty is that sense of anticipation, focused this time rather than ubiquitous. There were signs on the gates and fences and the side of the building that this was the Post Master General's property, and Her Majesty would have you hung, drawn and quartered if even so much as your gaze lingered on what little could be seen of the yard. It was truly a compound, first cousin to HM Prisons, a kind of *locus amoenus* of Britain's stake in the colonies, a foundational emblem. Once inside, you were in protective custody. Which meant you could lean your bike against the back wall of the Post Office and nobody would interfere with it. Unless, of course, they happened to work there.

And we hung around the back door, waiting for our orders – the habits of government offices are not much different from the habits of homesteads and fruit orchards, and both reach deep back into our colonial origins – and not knowing what to do until a postie with a big voice came out and roared at us to get inside and sign on quick and lively or we'd all be ruled off, whatever that meant. What it meant was that at 6.55 am the Head Postman ruled a double line across the time book, and anyone who signed on after that had his pay docked. What it also meant was that the big voice didn't belong to the Head Postman, who was above that. He didn't have to roar. The roaring was from a thickset underling who had unrealistic aspirations to do the ruling off. He was known as Buller.

The time book was a kind of sacred text. St Peter hadn't a more important account of us, a stricter measure of our lives. Everything was determined by that time book – not just the signing on, but more importantly, much more importantly, the signing off. The whole endeavour of the Christmas period was to build up the overtime; but there was an art to this, just like cheating on your tax. It is one of the authentic Australian art forms. Obviously you wouldn't want anomalies, you wouldn't want to draw attention to yourself – so you have to get your time up slowly, just as you steadily increase the amount of your claimed deductions. In the mail room the goal was that after seven hours and six minutes your rate of pay would change to time and a half for an hour and a half, then double time for the next two. And an office that really knew its business would aim for the jackpot, triple time. Yet you didn't want to overdo that because Head Office might decide to send out more assistance, and then there would be less work and less overtime to go around. But obviously, as the Postal Workers' Union had negotiated this top award rate, it was a possibility. It was there on the books; and you would be a mug if you didn't go for it. So a delicate balance had to be achieved, in getting what you could but without attracting undue scrutiny from the regional inspector, whose job it was to keep the posties up to the mark and to make sure that the overtime was held to a minimum.

What all this involved was elementary industrial psychology. Here the Australian worker was able to show some finesse. It wasn't just about rorting the system, though there are endless bloodyminded examples of that right across the community. More important was the manoeuvring, the cat and mouse game in which the worker finds an opportunity to display a modicum of imaginative flair, and through this to assert some measure of individuality deep inside the system that both gives and takes away his or her identity. In those years, his. It was partly a gamble too, a dash of risk-taking, and that in itself was an attraction. But you could always leave off, or cover the odds, go quiet for a bit. It was a satisfying annual ritual. And there was a further factor, of style – of not making a welter of it, and certainly not to make a fool of yourself, unless there was a tactical advantage in that. It made the whole game interesting.

But we knew nothing about all this. We had yet to learn how you really did this job. We had to wise up.

The basic skills were not too far beyond us. Big white canvas bags of mail – the smell of canvas and string dominated the entire sorting area – were emptied into a large yellowish bin, that putty colour which the government painted everything in those years, and the regular posties rough-sorted the letters into the different rounds. This was always a time of chiacking and riposte, when they performed for us, a wide-eyed audience. This was where they showed off and shared their knowledge – they really did know the movements of just about everybody in the entire suburb, and a good deal of gossip about them too. Contrariwise, they were merciless on any postie who made a mistake. Then the sorting into streets at each postie's desk, and little spurts of animosity between them would flare up, teasing that sometimes had a wicked edge to it. And all the time the radio was booming away, with Frankie Lane and Guy Mitchell and Perry Como. 'Amazing thing, the wireless – it goes on talking after you turn it off.' 'Yeah, just like Buller.' Sorting was a pleasant enough task. You had to keep in mind where each house was in relation to others, for it was immediately obvious that houses don't align themselves in neat numerical order, and the letterbox might be at one end of a front fence or the other, or in the middle; and you had to plan a route that took strategic advantage of the driveways. That was what the postie had to teach you; he had the optimum sequence written down in a book, but if there weren't any letters for some of the houses then you would want to re-arrange the sequence, so as to avoid criss-crossing the street unnecessarily.

And then it was a matter of loading the bundles of letters into a big leather bag strapped to your handlebars, and you were off. 'On yer bike, buster.' 'Ooroo uncle', and on that first day and for the next two or three the posties on their red low-slung PMG bikes and their attendant students on their own odds and sods – crates, we called them, or mangles – would peel out into the streets. 'Don't forget to wet your whistle,' one of them would call out. The point of the joke became clearer later on in the season. And at a leisurely pace the posties led us through the mazy round, stopping here and there for a cheeky exchange with elderly residents, chatting up the girls in shops and business offices – working up the round. Christmas was coming and it was a time for remembering the postie ... But it was also a time for a running sardonic commentary, drawing attention to those residents who were waiting for their mail, but were too hoity-toity to say g'day, pretending to be busy in their garden or hiding behind their screen doors, or twitching curtains; noticing a car parked outside that sort's house again and it's a bit early in the day for that sort of nonsense; warning about the bloody mongrel in the next house but one (and actually meaning a dog for once); and 'for Gawd's sake don't blow yer whistle till yer past Mrs Cawte's. If she nails yer, you'll never get to the other end of the street. Talk? She's got a mouth like a washing-machine'. It was an unwritten rule of course that the posties would never go slow on pension day.

In the next days, we were sent out on the special deliveries, the registered and certified mail, while the posties were putting the letters and streets for the entire round into order, leaving some sequences for us to deliver when we went round with them. That meant crossing dogs' territory and going to the front door; once, to the bedside of a man so feeble and trembling, and who signed for his registered parcel of documents with such a wavering X while I steadied the pen in his hand, that I was convinced he'd never live to sign anything else again. And I was sure that his mark was illegal since I had virtually written it myself. His hand going one way while I tried to make it go another reminded me of my father's determination once, when I was seven (the unwritten sequel to A.A. Milne), to sight along a rifle while I aimed at a bottle floating down the Murray. The more my father raised the barrel the more I pushed down, and the more he helpfully pushed it up again; in despair, with the gun waving around like Corporal Trim's stick, I pulled the trigger – and slowly, very slowly, a mortally wounded branch of willowtree buckled, fell into the river, and very nearly sank the bottle. I didn't feel that I had made my mark either.

And once there was a small registered packet for Balville Street. The posties knew exactly what that was about. They knew who lived there, and they were sure I was just the person to deliver it. They were setting me up. I would have to ring at the front door, and keep on ringing the doorbell, they told me, because it was for a nurse who worked the late shift and I would be getting her out of bed. And there was all sorts of additional oblique advice too.

I don't think I had ever met a nurse. I had seen them in British comedies, of course. And I had heard about nurses; by common report they were – what was the phrase? – progressive. Maybe that was just hopeful thinking. There I was, only the front door was open and the screen door was latched, so I couldn't reach the doorbell. I knocked and I knocked and eventually she came shuffling down the passage-way in her shiny petticoat and her slippers, slummocky and with a bent fag in her fingers, bruised-looking under her eyes and her hair just hanging anyhow. She was a character straight out of Patrick White. She was exhausted. She sagged more than she bulged. It was disconcerting to be that close to an under-dressed woman. It was still rare to see anything like that at the pictures, and as we didn't have television at home I can't report on what may or may not have been on display there – but in either case that wasn't close up and personal. She was not in the least bit interested. I had a red armband on identifying me as working for the Postmaster General, and I had a packet to deliver, and that was it. The posties pretended to be surprised that I was back so soon. There was mirth at what smart workers these students were, and the like. They were going to have their laugh whatever the case. But I was starting to see that their nudging and winking about the possibilities on their round was just talk, wishful thinking. More than that, a routine they all went through, not even a fantasy. Though for one or two that might not have been true. And then Elvis was on the wireless, the radio, singing the song they owned: 'Re-turn to sendah' the great one bawled, and they all joined in, stamping and snapping their fingers, 'ad-dress unknown'. And when that was finished, they'd all moved on from my little outing.

Smart work became the issue of the first serious step in our training. We were each allocated half a round, and we felt honour-bound to deliver our bundles of letters smartly, and get back to the Post Office promptly; and sign off, and return for the afternoon delivery. While there was just a regular volume of mail, nobody cared. You were going to be paid for a day's work, and if you could do it in a lot less time, good luck to you. But once the mail started to pick up, the serious business of building up the time sheets began. We didn't know this of course; it wasn't a thing that could be said. But a real worker would have known it automatically. Instead, we got to hear jibes about 'tear-arses', and we would be sent out with one registered letter at a time, return to the Post Office and be sent out with another. Obviously we weren't real workers, no matter how hard we tried – precisely because we were trying so hard. We had no idea, and we had no style. They tried to tell us, but we just thought they were joking – and so they were, much of the time. That was their way of keeping distanced from their work, keeping it in perspective, keeping themselves fresh and lively. They knew what was what, and they were comfortable with it. Being a postman, they said, is being right at the bottom of the pile. You can't be sent any lower because you're too old to be a telegram boy. So nobody expects you to work any harder than you do; and one way or another you've got it made. But we didn't pick up on what they were really telling us.

So came the morning we found our bikes had been tampered with. Our saddles had been raised higher, the chains were very tight, the tyres were soft, and I'm suspicious but I suspect the cone-nuts on the axle had been tightened. We didn't realise at first just how hard it was to pedal down the main road; we kept dropping behind, and we were much later back than the regular posties. Amazingly, they seemed rather pleased with us; kept telling us that we had made good time, but we misunderstood them. The next day was the first drift into overtime, just a half an hour by several of the postmen. They were on their way, and the Christmas mail would be delivered on schedule – meaning not before the official lunch break.

As the days passed we discovered there were various accepted strategies for building up time. Chatting sociably to whoever was waiting at the letter box. Checking your bundle of letters at the beginning of each street. Making sure your long socks were straight. Blowing your whistle before you pushed off to the next letter box, and blowing it often (it increased the chance of someone else at the gate further up the street). The sorting was taking longer too, even though you had by now become familiar with the sequences. A street full of letters got to be quite a handful, and it happened more often than you would think that the bulging wedges of letters between your fingers became too many to manage, and the letters splayed and spilled out and went, as the posties philosophically observed, dearie me, all over the place like a madman's shit.

There was not really anything in that to disturb the inspector. Hill, his name was, Hilly among the men, who like most Australian workers inveterately looked for two syllables and a demeaning, if not an infantilising, of names (Aussie, Brissie, Chrissie, Jonesy); and of course he had been a postie himself once. He knew most of the tricks of the trade. What most concerned him was the behaviour of the postmen outside the office, the more apparent lurks once they were out on their rounds, the potential public scandals. For example, one of the posties, Jimmy, had a park on his route, and the rumour was that he used to take a paperback with him and sit and read in the public toilet. He must have been doing something of the kind, because he had been a telegram boy and he still rode like a blue streak; he was enormously fit and his round was close to the Post Office. He could just about have been back before the slower ones had started. He was a bit wild, too – the others still laughed about the time he had swung around the mail room from one hanging fluorescent light to the next. And his best mate, Johnny, whispered that he had got two girls up the duff – but Jimmy just smirked. Who knows, maybe he had, or maybe he just attracted rumours. Or maybe he just listened to them.

If he was pretty quick one way, he wasn't too swift in another. The inspector went cruising the streets in his car, and had sprung him, reading a paperback in a public toilet. 'I've got to report you, Jimmy,' he said back at the mail room; 'and for God's sake next time park your bike out of sight, round the other side of the building. You're a bloody idiot.'

Hilly was a steel-haired, florid crusty character, tough talking – in fact he rasped, he didn't talk. But he was fair. Which left the posties in a moral quandary, as he was by definition the adversary, the Post Master General incarnate, or his henchman. Everything they did, everything that was done to them, was channelled through him. So you had to be suspicious, hostile, resistant. He was the enemy. But while none of them would admit to actually liking him – a man's got his self-respect after all, and besides you had to keep on working with your mates – it was evident that the inspector was okay. Still, like the law and parliament

and everything else in this country, you had to have an adver-
sarial system. That's how it had always been, and anything
different was unthinkable. As with so many of us, the posties
liked their social formulae stark and simple; they distrusted
complexities as too clever and therefore dishonest. Besides,
they knew how it really was – them against us. Which is a
telling phrase, for on the one hand it asserts solidarity while
on the other it concedes disadvantage. At best it is a boast
already making its excuses.

The inspector was after more worrying game. He wasn't
picking on the postmen at all, though they couldn't see that.
His role was to defend the integrity of a visibly public service.
One of his anxieties was with drinking. Our suburb was in
effect 'dry' – there were only two pubs in it, each right on
the boundary. It was a temptation at the warm end of the
year, especially as Christmas neared, to organise the delivery
so as to arrive at about lunchtime. That was bound to be
good for a beer; and as the tempo picked up, the more genial
barflies might also buy one for the postie … and it was not
unknown for one or two of the postmen to be so late back
from lunch that the afternoon delivery had already been
sorted. They'd be a bit cantankerous, and not inclined to
see the joke if anyone said something sidelong and flippant.
They had to deal with the telltale time book too. But their
wits weren't entirely fuddled. If Hilly turned up and looked
a minute or two at the telltale book, the book of revelation,
and then an even more intent minute or two at the malin-
gerer, the mail room would fall awfully silent, with only
Johnny Ray or the Platters intruding as everyone appeared
to concentrate on scrutinising unreadable addresses.

So where were you?

Out on me round.

Bit slow aren't yer?

Got a headache.

And what would that be from?

Sun most likely, Mr Hill.

And I suppose that's why you look sunburned. You should try wearing yer hat, blossom. Listen, I'll do you in if you try that on again. Get me?

Yes, Mr Hill.

The other posties didn't really approve of such blatancy. They all knew the rules; but worse, he wasn't pulling his weight. It was selfish; it was poor form, and it had no style. They weren't going to say anything about it of course; as far as possible they said nothing at all to the offender. To provoke them to say something to him, he'd become aggressive, start jeering at one or two of the others, so that there would be a collective defence and then everyone was at it again, and the difficulty had been eased over. But for the next few days he'd be called Sunblossom.

Sunblossom's next outbreak called for desperate measures. He'd been shouted so generously at the pub, just days before Christmas, that he'd forgotten the clock. The shock of the time almost sobered him up again, and the fast ride back to the Post Office – and there was the inspector's car. Back up the street he went, kicked in the spokes of his back wheel, and carried his bike into the yard. 'Had 'n accident Mr Hill – gotter fill in a report.' He got away with it that time. That had passable style. But he was sunk on the third time down – he was so drunk he fell off his bike and passed out (or perhaps it was the other way round) and some good Samaritan rang the Post Office. By the time he had been picked up, his face really was sunburned.

There was one postie though that the inspector was after; and it did seem to come down to something personal. Smithy was a grown-up version of the stinky boy at school.

He had nothing to recommend him. His hair stuck out like a dunny brush, his teeth splayed every which way too, he farted all the time or tugged at his crotch and he was irrevocably foul-mouthed. He was always going over to another postie to snigger up close to him. Or he was off to the toilets, to waste a bit of time – however he chose to do that. He didn't strike you as much of a reader. But he was touched as all of them were in some way or another by a crude notion of existential angst. He wholly accepted the story – no doubt apocryphal – about a postman who had gone for a bog and taken his time about it too; and after a long while the others had gone out to the toilets to chuck things at the door and to yell at him to get back to work – and found that he had died. 'Just think. Died with his pants round his ankles. Jeez.' He had died in fact like royalty, like George II, but that wouldn't have impressed mortality on Smithy as much as what happened to one of his own. For him, history had to be up close too.

His only interests seemed to be carnal, though in his case you would have thought that was a forlorn passion. You couldn't trust anything he said, including that his name was Smith; but he'd had a terrific time in Korea, really got into them – and he didn't just mean with his bren gun. It was nasty, the way he remembered his war effort. He made you shudder. Amazingly, he had a girlfriend, so to speak, on his round. Nobody believed this until the great debacle. The story, as we heard it, was that he'd spent so long with her one day that he left his undelivered letters at her place, wrapped up in a parcel, we heard later, intending to pick them up the next day and deliver them then. But he forgot, or she forgot or she wasn't at home when he called in and so another day went by and irritated residents waiting on promised mail started to ring in, all from one corner of the suburb – and then the cat was in among the pigeons, or out of the bag, or somewhere. There was one hell of a fuss; and a relieving postman was brought in. And 'Re-turn to sender, ad-dress unknown' the others all chorused, with shocking sardonicism. The group dynamic is merciless. Smithy's disadvantage was that he had never had a mate to protect his back, which is what you really need a mate for. He was just written off as a bludger.

Later there was an interesting turn to all this, an attempt by the workers to even up the score. While they didn't care that much for Smithy, they had to remind the management that it didn't get everything its own way. Someone, picking up a letter that had fallen to the floor, noticed an old chalk mark on the underneath side of their desk. Everything at the Post Office had a code number, even the sheets of toilet paper. So when the time seemed right, he called out to the inspector, 'What about getting us some 176Es?' 'Right, right,' said Hilly, 'I'll get on to it. Can't just think what that is at the moment, it'll come in a minute, it's on the tip of me tongue. How many do you need? A gross? Right …' and he bustled off making himself a note of it. There was enor-mous glee, and a bit of apprehension as they imagined the explosion when he twigged. The inspector was smart though. He did nothing and let them sweat on it. Maybe he waited until the students had all finished up.

And there was an ultimate confrontation about the time book. One of the posties hadn't signed off when the inspector surprised everyone by turning up late in the afternoon. The postie was back from his round, and messing around, letting the clock tick over for a few more valuable minutes. As was proper, the inspector started dressing him down. The postie – his name was Whitehead, which is why he was called Akker, acne, blackhead – startled us all by trying to grab it. But Hilly had a firm hold on the book, tucked tightly under his arm, and stepped round the other side of the sorting bins. His threat was real enough: a postman couldn't get paid for his time unless he signed off. postie started after it again, and suddenly there was a chase around the office. When the inspector thought he had sufficiently made his point, and read the riot act at Akker, and allowed him to sign in the time book, he had made an additional twenty minutes of overtime. Which had a few of the others whistling 'The Great Pretender' quietly through their teeth ...

It was not easy to know just where you stood in all this. Things said had such various spins on them. At any moment it could be an individual observation or a group point; it could be serious or a leg-pull or a set up. You certainly had to have your wits about you, and you had to be sensitive to nuance. Equally, you couldn't let yourself be over-sensitive. That constantly inconstant pattern of convergence and divergence requires some subtlety to perceive, let alone negotiate, and strangers haven't a chance. Mainly, they haven't a clue. Which is why it is so easy for Australians to take the mickey out of foreigners, especially those who think they speak English. And why it is so enjoyable to watch it happening.

Yet I wasn't quite sure how to take it when oblique talk about me joining them at their Christmas dinner started to float by. Obliqueness is habitual in the Australian vernacular – unless you want to disagree. Pig's bum. Bullshit. Rack off. Negotiating social occasions, though, can be a matter of diffidence, if not delicacy, just like handing on information. Likewise, you wouldn't want to be caught telling somebody how to do something if they already knew; they might know more about it than you do, you might be setting yourself up. Indirection is the go. In this instance, what if I hadn't wanted to go, what if I wouldn't be seen dead with that lot?

After all, I wasn't actually one of them. So the posties were sounding me out.

Most of the hotels were essentially workingmen's hotels; and for all that Adelaide is known as the city of churches, there were as in the other Australian cities many more hotels than churches. The workingmen knew where to find paradise. The old South Australian Hotel, with its famously and insistently snobbish maître de, Louis, aspired to a superior clientele, and it must have been an alarming contraindication when the Beatles stayed there. But there was no doubting the Zetland's ambient market. It catered for the workers. This was cut glass to crystal. We made an effort of course – we scrubbed up pretty well, in our jackets and ties and good shoes. We were there to spend a packet, to spend some of the overtime we had earned, and as we were still earning it right up to Christmas the dinner was held later, in January. Not to worry, the decorations were still up in the dining room. Indeed, they looked like they had been in place a good long while. Lots of rippled foil streamers and plastic holly – another of those garnered and not so exotic emblems – and a few limp balloons on long strings. Never mind that the carpet was a heavy brown, and the drape curtains dark, and the lighting dim and the band loud – we had ambience. And we had a table for nine, all good mates out on the town for the night. Well nearly all: there was a ring-in, a Pommie from the PO in the next suburb. There's always one to spoil a party.

Being a pub, no doubt there was roast pork and veg, just the thing for midsummer upstairs in an insufficiently ventilated hotel. And given the taste of the time, there could have been chicken Maryland, and something called tico tico which was bolognaise sauce on rice, demonstrating an international cuisine. We were learning heaps from our

New Australian friends. Obviously we must have eaten something. The reason for not being able to bring it to mind, however, is probably less to do with its lack of distinction than with the fact that we had each chipped in two quid for the drinks kitty. At nine shillings a jug, that would have bought forty jugs of beer, and nobody would have been able to count. The Pommie got to the stage of making disparaging remarks about Australian dining habits, and bought a round of Benedictine to finish the evening off. It did the trick.

We were well and truly primed. And the lads were getting restless. They had been looking around and there didn't seem to be much likely action – there were no tables of office girls, no nurses. There was the dance floor, and the band belting away, and more of the evening to get through. But over on the other side of the room was a table with a noisy lot of middling aged women who seemed to be having a good time. And one way and another everyone was soon up and dancing – we joined forces, and the dance floor was crowded and the sound picked up and the beat lifted and the party was swinging. Or maybe it was the beer and Benedictine chaser. I found myself dancing with a pleasantly plump woman, old enough to be someone's grandmother but determined to cut a caper a while yet. She was skittish, she was Scottish, she was hippy hippetyhop hopscotch – my head was in such a swirl I could hardly make any of it out. 'Where are you from dearie?' And for no good reason at all, just to be friendly I suppose, I invented another self. I may as well, as I seemed to have lost sight of wherever I started from. 'Ah coom frae a li'l pless no'th of Lunnen called Doomfrashier.' Maybe it was a better than passable imitation, or maybe she celebrated the intention; but there was a banshee shriek, I was hugged strongly and she planted a great kiss on me. And shockingly, her tongue was in my mouth, like the extruded centre of a sausage roll, some-how granular and dry, prodding, pushing. And immensely sobering. I was astonished. I had never experienced such a thing. This, after all, was in circumspect days, when movie kisses were invariably filmed from over the heart-throb's shoulder, with the leading lady's eyes closing in dreamy rapture; nothing like today's threatening encounter with the couple chewing each other's face off, or fishing with their tongues down each other's gullet. It felt like I had been vio-lated. And a whole new dimension of behaviour had been opened up. I remembered my manners of course; returned her to her friends, thanked her for the dance, headed back to the safety zone of the men's table, and anchored there. The power of illusion can be a terrifying thing. Ditto for disillusion.

It wasn't all over yet. We had booked taxis to get us back; they dropped me off at the corner of my street, sang out their farewells – 'See yer, mate', 'Ooroo, uncle' – and went on into the night. I'd arrived, but once again it wasn't where I thought I'd be. I had been accepted, and yet it was unlikely that I would have anything to do with them again. But I had been, if briefly, one of them. I had been united with the workers, I had been accepted as part of the brotherhood. Yet I also felt strangely detached from myself, in part because of the drinking, but more because in being one of them I had stopped being myself for a while. And I still had to stagger home; and I didn't feel very steady. Maybe, I thought, if I walk around the block I'll wear some of this off. I walked around the block a number of times, throwing up more often than anyone wants to read about. I should have been feeling desperately unwell, and my irresolutely suffering self was going to catch up with me the next day; but instead I was feeling oddly dissociated.

And I started to laugh, for I realised I had been singing to myself: 'In South Australia I was born, heave away, haul away'. Sick humour, I was thinking. Gag. Throwaway line. And I would have to face a different sort of music when I got home, and come clean.

8

Winter Games

'Come to sunny South Australia', the promotional literature used to say, and it wasn't all hyperbole. That was how we thought of ourselves, long before Queensland appropriated our trademark as its slogan; indeed, long before Queensland mattered, when Lennons was a solitary landmark in a low, windy and lacklustre belt of beach scrub, and the famous metermaids of Surfers Paradise still awaited the appearance, or possibly disappearance, of bikinis. Indeed, there were as yet no meters. Ours was the sunny state. The sunniness had baked itself into our very psyche. We were quite convinced that clouds massed up along the Victorian side of the state border, and did not dare trespass on our patch. Victoria, and Melbourne in particular, was mocked for its appalling weather: winter could strike at any time of the year. Cricket matches persistently were held up by rain, the odds were that the Melbourne Cup would be run on a heavy track. Winter conditions were such an entrenched feature of the Melbourne football season that Victorian football players developed a run-on style of play suited to muddy water-logged grounds, as distinct from the genteel kick and mark, kick and mark style of the South Australians. Truth to tell, Adelaide had its winters too, but at least its winter was not so dispiriting, and it was confined to the appropriate quarter of the year.

You could feel winter coming, from about two weeks after the football season started. And it finished at the end of the first week of the Royal Show; this when the Show ran for two weeks. You could see winter coming, as the light changed, and with it ideas of space and volume, as though the days were starting to close in, as indeed they were, but in a subtle way too, gradually shepherding us indoors. You could smell winter coming as the low scudding rainclouds moved in across pewter skies, over the bleached wheatstalks in paddocks still left on the Adelaide plains, north and south of the city, and across the open land over towards the coast. The first dampening of stubble and dry grass released into the air that completely distinctive smell of straw and settled dust, pungent yet slightly nutty, the equivalent somehow of the taste of the ubiquitous soursobs – and these were the sure and visible sign that winter was actually here, when their bright yellow flowers started to form. For curiously, winter is a succulent time of year. And you could hear the winter coming. On moonlit nights the galvanised iron roofs of the suburban houses creaked as the frost settled on them. When the clouds had gathered and the blustery west winds were up, then a way off, and then closer, came the drumming of the rain, drumming on the roofs and the chook-houses and garages and rainwater tanks and woodsheds and bike-shelters and beating against the fences, hammering on all that corrugated iron with the John Lysaght and Co. brand in the middle of each sheet, nearer and nearer until it was on your own roof and you could hear almost nothing at all for the roar and rattle of the first serious rains of the season, heavy as a hailstorm in sound effect.

And with winter, Adelaide went indoors, and lit its fires, and draped its damp pullovers and grey school socks over chairs and firescreens and clotheshorses.

Every house had its fireplace. They had to, because all the older houses – new houses were only just beginning to be built after the postwar restrictions had been lifted – had ventilators right through their double brick walls; or limestone or bluestone, depending on how old your house was. Whichever, you could see through the ventilators the twinkling stars in the frosty night sky, and that didn't make for snug, whatever it was meant to contribute to moral fortitude. My Australia wasn't all about bronzed Aussies and suntans; there was the chilblain factor too.

Adelaide's firewood was at this time all but invariable. If you hunted about you could get lengths of stringy-bark; but mostly you ordered in a load of mallee, short lengths of the slender trunks and branches which had to be split lengthwise. But not the hollow logs, which burned from the inside out and were just the thing for getting a fire to really draw. And you ordered in mallee stumps, gnarled and knotted, which burned slowly and generated huge heat; and these could only be split into manageable chunks by using a sledgehammer and wedge. It wasn't uncommon for a corner of the wedge to become bent or even to snap off, so tough was that wood. The logs and the stumps were brought by rail from the endless scrub country and in to the city, and at certain places the railway yards would have small mountains of these, piled up for the winter season. At a later date we were encouraged to buy briquettes, slipper-sized and made of compressed Leigh Creek coal. At school, we were taught that it was soft brown coal, insignificant by comparison with the hard black coal of the eastern states. But it was black, it left black on your fingers, its soot was black. And even if it was an industrial and pedagogical embarrassment, it was ours and we could do something practical with it. There didn't seem to be anything else that soft coal was good for. It left a lot of ash, and it didn't burn as well as mallee. But it represented progress and manufacture, it had been processed, and no doubt the premier, Tom Playford, had appealed to our moral sense of the inherent virtue of that industry. As though gathering mallee did not represent sufficient independence and labour.

Five, six, pick up sticks. Seven, eight, lay them straight. All over Adelaide the chimneypots were smoking. The washing, which would never dry in the damp air between rain squalls, was draped on clotheshorses around the fires and made a kind of domestic cave or a Bedouin's tent, as your fancy chose. And in there you could read books or toast crumpets, or weave? knit? sew? long multicoloured and wholly useless cords of wool, doing tom-boy stitch on four or five nails tapped into the end of a wooden cotton-reel. There didn't seem to be any point to this, apart from the pleasure of doing it. No tom-boy stitch was ever finished; the instructions were all about process, not completion. As for purpose, it was suggested you could use these as pyjama cords, or dressing-gown cords, but that never happened. If you had got to grade five, you might try your hand at knitting or tapestry, but if you were only in grade four you sewed woollen threads in various patterns on a piece of hessian bagging, in and out and criss-crossing in as many kinds of coloured lines as pleased your constrained and automatic eye. Sewing was the issue, not artistry. There were board games that could be played underneath the dining-room table if the floor-space inside the flannelette wigwam was too crowded. Or you could just stare into the bright orange embers, your face too hot, your eyes and cheeks bright, and do your dreaming there, rather than in the chill bedroom that awaited you.

My grandfather's fireplace had brass boxes with padded hinged seats at each end of the fender; kindling and bits of newspaper and the matches were kept in one of them. As he had a separate coal scuttle, anything might have been in the other box, stray pieces from a draughts board or bits of string or a stub of pencil. And the fire screen was dimpled brass, and had a sailing ship in full sail hurling across fixed rampaging seas just like I could see from the sleepout whenever I stayed there, and sat up in bed peeping below the blind. In the famous winter storm of 1953, the seas were distinctly bigger than any Tudorbethan brass ship encountered. These were big menacing waves that crashed over the sea-wall, hollowed out the landfill behind it, gouged out the sand from around the roots of massive Norfolk Island pines, took the decking and the rails off the jetties and then skewed their pylons.

The big beach shelters were never seen again. The pounding seas undermined the corner of the municipal swimming pool, and the diving tower had to be dismantled. Days afterwards, these were still big clay-coloured waves with white suds down their front, and they bore in on the coast with malice aforethought. They're arranged the coastal geography. They washed sand away from the beaches near the Port and dumped it all in the mouth of the Torrens. And when they had done, they left stranded on the beach pungent reefs and atolls and islands of seaweed, smelling like old urine, or old mattresses, and uprooted sponges and all sorts of flotsam and jetsam, and we clambered atop these, higher than ourselves, jumping over channels and gulleys and ravines. Years later panic flew about the beach suburbs that another such storm was imminent; some even said a tidal wave, but the premier of the day promised if necessary to stand at the end of the reconstructed Glenelg jetty and command the waters to be still. The mere promise had its own calming effect on the electorate. Maybe he reckoned he could walk on water too, the more caustic of the disbelievers commented. Though given the notorious hardness of South Australian water, that did not represent much of a challenge.

The firescreen we had at home had a pair of hunting dogs, a most unlikely motif in our largely dogless household. With a serial menagerie of everything else, from a Norwegian rat to a thorny devil, from a budgie to silkworms to, just briefly, a bat, a dog would have been, well, a bit obvious. There was no need for a dog then. That firescreen belonged to the diningroom fireplace. The screen in the front room represented style; it was a brass wire screen in a very moderne frame.

There were tongs for picking up embers, and a brush like a German general's moustache – or the cartoon version of such a moustache – and just as useless at its duty, and a brassy dustpan that disappeared at some stage; and best of all, a poker. No fireplace was complete without a poker. No fire was good without poking. And it was the absorbing process of poking at the fire that resulted in an arc of scorch marks on the carpet just in front of the hearth, where sparks might fly with no screen to prevent them. If you got the poker hot you could use it to accelerate burning out the core of any mallee log which had been attacked by ants, so that the fire would draw right through it. If you got the poker hot enough you could burn your name into the bark of one of the logs. Log is an immoderate word, but it is what we used, just as we spoke proudly of Mount Lofty when it is no more than an undistinguished peak in the long, low range of the Adelaide Hills. We made do with what we had. Prodding at the glowing coals may have been an inherited addiction as one of my forbears had been a blacksmith, unlikely as that antecedent was given the family physique. The past does not lie; it just embarrasses us. The past declares its distinction, and that is not a claim we can make for ourselves.

If it was Sunday, we lay on the carpet by the fire and listened to the radio serials and 'Under the Stars' and later, if the program was suitable, a radio drama. But sooner or later we had to head for bed, and bedrooms were designed for summer living. The chill floated just above the linoleum floors. And a zone of cold hovered just inside the window panes. There was plenty of fresh air and ventilation, draughts came in from underneath doors and around the edges of the windows. Just about every house had a sleep-out, a home-made extension at the back of the house (except for my grandfather's, where what was called a sleep-out was actually a glassed-in sun-room at the front of the original house and looked directly across the promenade to the sea). No sleep-out ever won an architectural award. Sleep-outs were not designed for capaciousness. They were a suburban equivalent of shearers' quarters: room for two single beds with sagging meshed wire bases, a bit of a walkway between them, and a wardrobe at one end. Cotton candlewick bedspreads of course. Walls that may not quite reach the ceiling – tendrils of grapevine curled into mine, and occasional large brown spiders with them, but not in the winter months. A pull cord dangling from the ceiling for the light. There was something forlorn about that pull cord. This was not a comfort zone. This was for developing fortitude. You piled whatever you could find on to the bed – dressing-gown, jumpers, anything to add a few layers of warmth. You kicked off your briquette-shaped slippers, possibly bought at Barlows in the city, just along from Beehive Corner, where there was an x-ray machine in a cylindrical wooden stand and when you put your foot in an opening and peered into another opening at the top, you could see the pallid silhouette of your toes wriggling in an eerie green light, the green light of medical specimens and aquariums and Ghost Trains and the Emerald City, and strange dreams.

You left your socks on to keep your feet warm in bed. And you sank into the boat-shaped hollow of your mattress and listened to the smack and spat of rain on the window panes, and the gusting wind and the rattling frames, and the drumming on the iron roof, and the spouts of water overflowing from the rainwater tank. And in no time at all, the next sound you heard was the shed door being pulled open and your father going in to make up some warm bran and pollard for the hens, and it was another morning.

Winter as remembered is defined mainly in terms of weekends. At school, you were hardly alive. At school you learned long division and the textile manufactures of the state and the solfa scale and whatever else was necessary. We didn't get to learn anything interesting, like how those notes got their name from a Latin hymn to St John. We learned grammatical rules, but not the reasons that gave rise to them. Nothing was *explained*. School was only formative in the way educationists like to think of it. Real formation has to do with lived experience and imaginative engagement, if that doesn't sound too much like the sort of thing educational psychologists say. School is not life, though it takes up a large proportion of it. You absorbed what was taught, but it didn't require any effort, it offered no experience. The polio epidemic came and went, and with it the boy who shared your desk. A teacher died in a motor-bike crash, we got a new spelling primer each year, we learned how to write in running writing and the importance of down-strokes. Nothing was more or less important than anything else; there were no degrees of light or shade at school. Just abstract certainties.

Outside school, we took advantage of whatever opportunities there were. We rode our bikes around the streets, gradually probing further and extending our local knowledge, but without straying into the next suburb, and never ever going down by the railway line, which represented some kind of taboo border rather than a danger to life and limb. There was something morally untidy about the sorts of activities that went on down by the railway line apparently. Unquestionably. The more effective constraint was that if you did go down that way you had a very steep long hill to come back up.

We rode our bikes to the parklands where the Golden Crust Bakery horses grazed, fenced in by three-strand wire fences, and where notices on the infrequent gates prohibited cows. All across the playing fields and especially along the occasional ditches, soursobs and onion grass and rogue clumps of Scotch thistle flourished, and galahs shrieked and magpies whistled. We would kick a misshapen football about, or a wet heavy soccer ball, and tie lengths of damp grass in knots to see if someone might catch their foot and fall over. Australian rules. But the light did not last for long, and we would soon have to get on our bikes, and head for home, and put our shoes in front of the fire; and our jumpers and socks smelled like, well, like wet wool. There is no smell like that, though you could get close to it by chewing string.

Or for a more impressive sortie, sometimes we would ride up to the local oval and watch the first-grade league footy team practising. What we really did was scout around the ground, up in the grandstand or at the back of the spectators' mounds, looking for empty soft drink bottles. We could get a couple of pence refund for each one we returned, and it didn't take long to build up a small nest-egg. But we had to establish a cache, as the drinks stall was only open on Saturdays when there was a home match. We reckoned we had found a good place up in a poplar tree, where we had built a crazy kind of platform for vantage viewing; but a groundsman or maybe an envious someone from a rival gang, if that is what we were, pulled down the platform not knowing what else was up there, and left a tell-tale litter of broken glass at the base of the tree. Our stock-pile had crashed. We were wary of going near that tree again, in case we were being watched; but it meant that we weren't going to feast up on pies and Woodroofe's sarsaparilla as planned. Cowley's pies, more likely than Balfours'; Balfours was establishment, and their products were for savouring, not guzzling. Rosella tomato sauce of course.

This was a time for collecting cigarette cards. Actually we didn't understand what that meant. The nearest equiva-lent to these were caricatures of football players with large heads and tiny bodies and in their team uniforms, that used to turn up on match-box sized cards inside boxes of rolled oatmeal. But we had read in British annuals about collecting cigarette cards, and translated this as meaning collecting covers from all the different cigarette brands – Ardath, Craven A, Capstan in their different colours, orange, blue, red, De Reschke, Turf, Lucky Strike … Mid-week was a good scavenging time, and the pickings were extraordinary. Everybody smoked at the footy matches. All the ex-diggers in their blue suits and broad-brimmed hats would pack the mounds, straining and swaying in tandem with the action out on the field, a smouldering fag hanging from their lip. A goal was an opportunity to fumble out their packet to light up another. At half-time they'd go off and have a pee, and buy a beer and then get back to their spot. The whistle blew and up went the ruckmen, 'Cats' Carroll against 'Candles' Thompson, and the diggers would be leaning and twisting with them in some kind of shared tension, elbows and feet jerking. And there were old codgers re-living the glory days they had never had, twitching and squirming with the play, even stab-kicking into the forward pocket when the lead was offered. They were all rapt in the restless cross-currents of play, gasping at adventurousness, and again at crunching contact, sighing at missed opportu-nity, and roaring in protest at any perceived wrong-doing, whether by player or umpire. It was as much an occasion for voicing outrage, for demanding fairness, as it was about par-ticipating at a remove in athletic skill, following the play. Unlike justice, the umpire was not meant to be blind, and the crowd let him know it. Their anger at foul play was in moral terms too. 'Bludger' they would shout, and boo; they weren't much fussed about legitimacy, but about right and wrong. And in all the excitement they threw down their empty cig-arette packets and their empty bottles and at the end of play left the field to active and discerning small scroungers.

You could always get into the oval for free after three-quarter-time, when the gates were thrown open. But there was usually a gate open behind the stands, and you never knew, the keeper might give us a wink and let us through to the terrace. There was no way you could convince the gatekeepers your dad was waiting for you up in the stands. Anyway, it was colder up there, and you couldn't move around so easily, looking for the empties before some other kid found them.

Sometimes, if we were early enough, we were allowed in under the stands, allowed to stand in the doorway of the changing rooms where the players were flinging their locker doors about, and talking in big voices to each other and some of them were lying on long tables and being slapped about by the masseur, and the whole place reeked of liniment and leather boots. You were embarrassed to look too closely, but some of the players weren't wearing much more than a strange arrangement of elastic bands; others wore a pair of bathers (we didn't call them 'togs': that was the idiom of Melbourne and *Boys' Own Annuals*. And as for 'cossies' . . . ridiculous!) and more than a few looked distinctly flabby, pastry-coloured, hardly in the pink of condition. They carried the sort of weight you'd expect to see on chump challengers in a sideshow boxing tent. Some-one was checking the sprigs on the players' boots, banging in any protruding nail heads; yet when the team ran down the tunnel, along the concrete ramp and out on to the field, you could hear the metallic scratch and clatter which suggested he may have missed a few. And there was a great cheer from the crowd, and the ringing hollow thump as the players kicked a few tightly inflated footballs about – unlike the dead soggy balls we used in the parklands – and then the umpire gave his distinctive whistle call, the sirens blared and it was on; and we rushed out the back of the stands and around to one or other end of the oval, as close to the goalposts as we could get, as close to the yellow picket fence, where you could hear the grunt of the players and the tearing of their sprigs in the turf.

The oval belonged to the district. It was the centre of various community activities. Across the road were the Memorial Gardens, just as at the Adelaide Oval. Nearby was a Mothers and Babies, not at all a convenient location, in a part of the suburb by that time noticeably free of prams. The baby boom no longer happened in the streets of Federation era bungalows, but in the less pretentious, more affordable cottages in the newer, remoter streets of the suburb. There was a fenced playground, with old-fashioned see-saws and swings and a rotunda where teas were no longer served. Those facilities were markers of an earlier, sedate and comfortable era, and waited on more affluent days for their revival, or re-development. There was a bowling club with the grass browned off and top-dressed, a study in perspective and still life; and asphalt netball courts which doubled as tennis-courts in the summer. From time to time the oval was the venue for some momentous occasion. Once, the Chinese national soccer team played Australia there. And once Dave Sands gave an exhibition bout.

That was an occasion of considerable local anticipation. We didn't get much of a chance to see champions of any kind in Adelaide. Although boxing was distinctly déclassé, all the dads used taking their boys as an excuse to step outside their routine working lives. This was a midweek evening event; we could sit in the stands – only a stranger would find that a difficult phrase – and everything had the thrill of novelty. We were bundled up in our warm best coats, we had scarves to keep our ears warm. The boxing ring was set up just inside the picket fence, and lighting had been rigged up above it. None of the ovals had floodlighting then, and the last minutes of some of the football matches were played in an encircling gloom. Apart from the ring itself, this exhibition bout was in almost total darkness, just a few weak light-bulbs here and there.

There were some uninspiring preliminary bouts between hopeless amateurs, or so the man behind us complained. Mere slap and tickle. Some wrestlers in the sort of bathers that footballers wore beneath their shorts were more lively. And then the moment we had been waiting for: 'Ladies and gentlemen …!' It was understood that ladies would steer clear of an event like this, but the courtesies were to be observed. 'I give you …' and Dave Sands in his green satin dressing gown, and his brother in blue I think, climbed casually into the ring. And they just stood toe to toe and had a training session. What? No circling referee cautioning against low blows, no attack and defence, no ducking and weaving and dancing back out of reach? It was unbelievable. After five or six minutes of that they stopped, and put on their shiny dressing gowns, waved to the stunned crowd, clambered down and disappeared into the darkness. Well what else would you expect from New South Wales? Rope-able, the man behind us said he was. Since that time I've always associated the word with boxing rings. Everyone had the same view of the proceedings; and in that perverse and unexpected way, the hidden ties of community were reinforced once again. That was possibly the year that Parsons, the man next door, gave us boxing gloves for Christmas, but it was too late. I thought about it later and decided I could understand what had happened. You wouldn't want to thump your brother too much. I had brothers of my own and knew how chancy that would make your life.

The deep midwinter was rarely marked. The fog would be terrible up in the Hills, especially on the road leading down from the Eagle on the Hill to the Devil's Elbow, and there would be accidents of varying degrees of seriousness. But once every five or six years there might be the lightest dusting of snow up on Mount Lofty, so justifying its elevated name. The bush telegraph worked in the city too; families would drive up to the Summit to see for themselves before the snow disappeared, to fill their thermos with scrapings of snow, to throw small handsful of compressed slush at each other. Next day the front page of the *Advertiser* would carry a large black and white photograph of all this excitement, pretty much in true colour. It continues to do this on each rare occasion that snow falls, a part of the repetition of communal experience that becomes over time an established if intermittent event, and reasserting by its unvarying report the spirit of shared play, something like a great big picnic, something everybody knows, everybody has access to.

The Hills provided opportunities for other spontaneous collective activities according to the season, a bit like spawning only more respectable. At the right time, some-where in the transition from hot to cool, dry to damp, all along the Gorge Road the great bursting hedges of wild blackberries were ripening, and again as by some tribal instinct families would arrive by the carload, and plunge with their billies and buckets into the bushes. It gave 'heading for the Hills' a whole new definition. For the littlies, this was just so much finger food, easy pickings. For the bigger children, it was a chore and a pleasure and a competition, and an interruption to the tadpoling that could be done in the trickling creek, eventually a river, on the other side of the road. For the grown-ups, it was an earnest business, representing maybe a dozen jars of blackberry jam. And for everyone, there was a picnic afternoon tea, the children permitted to have sweet milky tea with their rock-buns and Anzac biscuits and fruit-slice and cup-cakes. And then it was time to pack everything away, and pile into the car, and join the long slow queue of traffic all the way down the narrow winding road, down the slopes and into the suburbs, with everyone playing 'I spy' and occasionally arguing with each other and slowly falling silent and sleepier and sleepier.

Early in the season, with the advent of winter, it was time to go mushrooming. Adelaide had not sprawled very far. On the other hand, the roads were narrow and the driving more sedate, so any expedition was as venturesome as more distant destinations these days. We headed *en famille* out to the lush green paddocks of Modbury and Golden Grove and Tea Tree Gully. Here and there along the road out that way were occasional Scotch thistles standing above the stubble. Somewhere the road had an intriguing kink around a solitary hotel, and you wondered about the surveyors' lunch-break. And there was a forlorn Adelaide plains gumtree which had avoided being turned into so many fence-posts, an emblematic last survivor of its race. This anomaly wasn't what gave One Tree Hill its name, though it might have. Everything out this way was a one-off, dramatic and significant because there was no other within cooee.

We were headed for a brick church somewhere out there, comparably isolated, without a community, a plain building with a tin roof and a big galvanised iron rainwater tank at the back and we knew where the tap lever was hidden so we always had water to make tea. It was right out on its own, in the middle of nowhere, with a country gate you unchained so we could park out of sight, behind the intermingled clumps of boxthorn and blackberry, out of sight so as not to give anyone else the same idea. And through the strands of wire we had vast open fields to ourselves, and in among the succulent green grass huge mushrooms nestled, big as plates and as white, big as cow pats and equally corrugated brown beneath. In fact, a good many had been stupid enough to try to grow up beneath or through a cowpat; or so close as to have been spattered. We dared each other to pick some of those and put them in the basket but of course there was always the possibility that that's the one you might get on toast tomorrow. If you could find a dry enough pat you could whack it with a stick to see it explode into a cloud of dust; or if it didn't disintegrate, flick it at whoever was near-by. If cows had been native to Australia, lacrosse could have been invented here.

As we got older, these family outings got more difficult to manage. We started to do our own different things, play soccer or the new sport recently arrived from America, baseball. Netball for girls. Besides, the suburbs were starting to spread out in the direction of the mushroom paddocks, more and more people seemed to know about them, and didn't seem to need the key to the rainwater tank behind the church. One custom seems to encapsulate the kind of inevitable change that was taking place, bravely asserting its ritual continuity but helpless against the new external pressures that were mounting. Like a good many families in those days, we all went to church on Sunday mornings. And because that meant the weekend roast could not be put on in time, the roast dinner was re-assigned to Saturday. The weekend was not defined unless there was a roast dinner; a woman was failing her duty if lamb and thick brown gravy and three veg didn't get dished up. And it was a midday roast, a great leg of hogget from the cool-room at the back of the butcher's shop, where the carcasses of sheep and beef hung from a heavy metal rail, carried in from the abattoirs truck by men in strangely medieval garb, a kind of grubby grey cotton hood and short cape.

The tradition of the roast dinner no doubt had its origin in England (I can't ever recall anyone saying 'Home' though you read that people said it). But it made sense in Australia, where meat was plentiful. If anything, it echoed more the old days than the old country. It was appetising, it was filling; and it gave you the stitch if you went to play soccer afterwards. Gradually the rule of the roast waned, but not the persistent fact itself. If as often enough happened the roast wasn't quite done and you were running late for the match, you were permitted to shave a few slices off the leg and take whichever of the vegetables seemed somewhere near cooked, and eat that ahead of the others. Season by season, as though anticipating the exodus of the von Trapp family, there would be fewer and fewer of us sitting down at the table, more and more scraped dishes left in the kitchen sink. And versions of that were happening everywhere. What was meant to have been the main meal of the week atrophied, got stranded. Entrenched custom carried a value in itself, as custom. It had a status almost as iconic as the Roman lares and penates. It was frequently an unwelcome because inappropriately heavy meal, and yet in retrospect there is a strange kind of reassurance in the memory of it, in the recognition that this was familiar practice. We outgrew it, but subsequently came to re-value it. It was a common domestic event, and although the specific act of sharing was limited, the common recognition of it becomes a kind of activity, and value, that both shapes and defines community.

One winter I was in no great hurry to leave the table, as I had been somehow inveigled into 'doing jobs' on Saturday afternoons for what would now be called a pensioner, living on a pittance in a little cottage a mile or two away, a long enough ride in light drizzle. I think this was meant to be some kind of character-improving activity for me. I got paid, but so little that I resented it, and that undid all the charitable warmth I suppose I was meant to be feeling. I just felt wet and cold. I hacked into the unyielding rammed earth that was meant to be her garden, I grubbed out antique bamboo from the chook pen, I pruned trees, I got up on the laundry roof and replaced a sheet of iron with a sky-light – that was a very cold day. And she kept watching me from the kitchen window the whole of the afternoon, to make sure I was earning my few shillings. Though South Australia has no convict experience, it was easy enough at times like this to identify with it. Maybe she can be defended as necessarily frugal, and no doubt her circumstances were meagre; but there was a meanness in this too which incensed me, and a rapaciousness which shocked me. And a moral predicament, as I tried to justify to my parents, at the end of that season of discontent, why I was withdrawing from doing good works. I could think of better ways to spend my Saturday afternoons. They had all the easy points to make, but they hadn't experienced the discomfort of riding into a headwind with drifting sleet all the way home after a freezing and bone-tiring afternoon out in the bracing fresh air.

In colder climates, winter is set aside for social activities (dashing through the snow, in a one-horse open sleigh etc). For us, it was a much more limited program, of visiting and being visited – again, a mere shadow of more elaborate social patterns in older, more established countries. We sometimes went visiting on Sunday afternoons, to grandparents or great aunts. Not often; mostly we went to Sunday School. There was a comparative absence of great uncles, not because of Lone Pine and Vimy Ridge though that may have had something to do with it. It may also account for the numbers of maiden aunts in that generation. The widowed aunts had a more recent history. Such matters weren't part of anything we heard talked about. Mostly it was a case of being measured for the next cable-stitch jumper that was being knitted for us, and then being told to go and play in the garden but don't climb in the trees, and to come in when we were called for scones and cream and blackberry jam ('Mum, that's the jam we gave her'). One great aunt we especially loved wore tiny pointed low-heeled shoes with buckles, like a dainty pirate. Or somebody might come to visit us, and that was a business of shining the entire silver service on the traymobile, and filling the sugar basin and the salt and pepper shakers which had been empty since last time in case of corrosion, and vacuuming the carpet and sweeping the fireplace; and it also meant lots of activity in the kitchen, and mixing bowls to scrape out and beaters to lick.

One way or another, winter worked through its recognised pattern. All too quickly the football season arrived at its inevitable climax, the Grand Final. In fact, it is a peculiar characteristic of winter sports in general that they come to a resounding conclusion. Summer sports don't seem to arouse anything like the same interest in finals and grand finals. Summer lingers on, as though it doesn't have to finish. Winter is hard pressed, there is a dash to it. The football finals were always played at the Adelaide Oval, a bigger and better version of our own. Bigger stands, larger crowds, more empty bottles but more competition for them. Fewer trees: there was, there still is a group of Moreton Bay figs at one end where you could get up in the branches and have a terrific view down the length of the ground. But bigger kids, supporters of the rival team (invariably Port Adelaide, so they were tough as well) would have taken possession, or dispossessed anyone else, so that we had to content ourselves with the possibility of a more extensive range of cigarette packs, along the terraces and down in front of the grandstands. A decade later, the innocence of all that disappeared with two children ...

In the backyards of the suburban houses, the cuttings

from the fruit trees and the vines and other garden rubbish had been accumulating in a large pile; and as a last vestigial rite, the season was farewelled with a bonfire. At dusk, with all the chores done (we said 'jobs' in the days before America started seeping across our culture), we'd shove screwed up sheets of the *Advertiser* in among the twigs, and if everything was damp there might even be a splash of petrol tossed on to the pile; and as the flames took and built and the smoke started drifting across the yard we'd all slowly gather there, staring into this fire just as we had been doing inside all through the rainy months, but knowing the difference this one signalled. This time we were out of doors. Sparks carried up in the plume of heat, branches burned through, shifted, collapsed and re-arranged themselves in the deepening bed of red hot coals, and someone would think of cooking potatoes in the ashes, and then and there, under the stars, we would know that this was the last of the dark side of the year, that the subsiding fire was dramatising a change in the air, a return to our more expansive world. This was luxury, indulgence; this was not heat we needed to warm ourselves though we would keep close enough to it. The iron fences reflected the flickering light, but with it you could still sense waves of chill. The bonfire was a kind of declaration that the time of cold and wet was over. In gathering around the fire we were undoubtedly re-enacting, unaware, a rite equivalent to those of more distant cultures and societies. If so, it was a ritual of our own devising. Like all those other patterns and customs, ultimately it did not matter where they came from, nor perhaps what they expressed. Much more important was that these little actions, repeated again and again across the community, were what in fact identified it as a community, a group sharing such patterns of experience. There was nothing particularly profound about any of it, nothing sophisticated. But there was social cohesion, and local attachment, and a kind of kinship. As there has always been around low warm fires glowing in the friendly dark.

9

The Big Smoke

Interstate. The way we understood that was as an absolute proposition. Interstate implied no reciprocity; it was a one-way deal, and usually not a very good one. Bad water came – comes – down the river from interstate and it stayed here. Those who went interstate mainly did not come back. To go interstate meant to re-locate rather than to visit. Interstate was the title of our book of Exodus.

In particular, interstate meant Melbourne; for the adventurous, Sydney. And those were places to be wary of, places of sharp practice and dubious morality, of St Kilda and Kings Cross and crooks and rampaging Catholic archbishops, and overweening assumptions of self-importance based as far as we could see on a romantic fabrication of historical accident. Something like that. They made a big hoo-ha about convicts and bushrangers and goldrushes, but what was so special about any of that? That wasn't anything they had invented, like the stump-jump plough; that was merely what had happened to them. They didn't make history, but they reckoned they owned it, all of it. They were the big-timers in the East, and they were a long way away.

Our hidden intuition was not that they didn't matter, but that perhaps, collectively, we didn't. The inverse of interstate was the parochial loyalty of being South Australian, a curious label when you thought about it. The name specifically identifies the state as less than the whole, a constant humbling reminder. At the same time, it is the wrong name: Tasmania is properly the southern state. And as at an early stage South Australia stretched all the way north to Darwin, it is difficult to imagine what on earth our forbears were thinking of. The West signified a proper longitudinal slice of the whole continent; South is a contingent latitude, at cross purposes, one would think, with the moral determinations of the founding fathers.

Constant humbling is an irritation, and it did Victorian relations with South Australia no lasting good that they kept defeating our state team in interstate football matches; even less, that our best players got tempted into playing in the VFL. South Australians will still barrack strenuously for any team that looks like it might beat a Victorian team. New South Wales was a different matter. It didn't play Australian Rules so there was more tolerance of it. Its cricket team occasionally overwhelmed the state side at the Adelaide Oval, but the local reflection was that our boys were effectively up against the national eleven so that it wasn't a proper match. The real point was that Sydney was so far away it might as well be in another country. It was at the remote edge of the continent, the other side of the back of beyond. We didn't understand the illogicality of its stranglehold on Broken Hill, when all the ore came down to the Whyalla smelters, and all the miners and their families came down to Largs Bay for their holidays. Broken Hill ran on South Australian time, and we were quite prepared to think of the people there as ours. We were not thinking in terms of revenue, obviously. Melbourne could be reached in a long day's drive provided you survived the gauntlet of the speed-cops round about Kaniva and Nhill, a division specifically set up to nab South Australian drivers, accustomed to a higher speed limit than that in the other states. That was one of the few acknowledged measures of our innate superiority. Or, perhaps, of the flatness and straightness of our roads.

Victoria was, of course, not an altogether unknown entity. Numbers of singers used to go across to the Ballarat eisteddfod (still at that stage occasionally spelled and therefore pronounced Ballaarat), a cultural oasis at a safe enough distance from Melbourne. Once we went on a caravan trip to Hall's Gap, in May, and the ice on the car windscreen was half an inch thick. Melbourne itself was renowned for Kooyong and 'Chloe' in Young and Jackson's bar and that was pretty much it, apart from the recent Olympic Games, which I suppose was our first experience of virtual reality though we didn't know it then. We could see bits and pieces of the Games on the brand new medium, television, with the signal bounced off a DC3 circling above Nhill. I doubt whether the pilot was able to watch, so that must have been a mind-numbing shift for him. There is not a lot of drama in the Wimmera landscape.

As with any order of experience, knowledge about is not the same as knowledge of. At some stage, our growing up as Australians ('I am an Australian, I promise Chifley to obey his laws' we had intoned at assembly in primary school) required us to take on larger familiarities – not specifically to encounter Melbourne and Sydney, so much as taking our own measure against the perspective of the more or less new. This was a different order of experience from that celebrated regularly at every major port around Australia, the P&O liner freighting yet another cohort of young Australians on the great adventure to Colombo and the Suez Canal and ultimately London, severing ties as gently and as absolutely as the skeins of twisted coloured streamers that momentarily linked ship and shore. Going interstate, we weren't leaving home, and yet we were. And changes of perception would be inevitable. It was a trial period in which we would experiment with being responsible for ourselves.

It was not exactly a rehearsal for leaving the nest. That kind of flight is ultimately a solo experience, like swimming across the Murray. In this case, we went as a group, a sports team; we knew each other and could take whatever reassurance we might need from that. On the other hand, we did not need to know each other any better than the team activity required. We carried with us common assumptions but likewise enough separateness to allow us each our own version of whatever the experience was to be.

The cheap way to travel was to take the train, the overnight Melbourne Express, sometimes called the Overlander though that name might seem to have more to do with droving. Given sufficiently well-patronised carriages, you didn't have to work hard to find a parallel. Because of its length, the Melbourne Express had its own dedicated platform. It was in fact quite an elegant train service, with dining cars and sleeping cars and baggage vans, and a First Class and Second Class and nobody to take any socialist offence at that, it was just two different grades of service; and guards and porters everywhere. And as with the P&O, so with the Overlander, there were always friends and relations to see everyone off.

Of course we were excited at the imminent adventure. We were all there perhaps a little earlier than was altogether stylish, but you didn't go interstate every day of the week. Our excitement was met right at the outset, in a way we had none of us anticipated. One of the team, comparatively unknown to the rest of us, had I later realised interested himself to take advantage of the travel arrangements, though we thought he was there to help make up our numbers. He was German, from Germany not from the Barossa Valley, and he flaunted his difference. He arrived almost late, wearing a greatcoat draped over his shoulders, and a long scarf, and that struck the rest of us as tremendously stylish. He was tall, and had long straightish fair hair; a kind of thin-faced Hal Porter sans moustache. And just as theatrical. And he was being farewelled, ardently embraced, by a smashing piece, equally tall and theatrical in her dress. She gave him a single long-stemmed red rose, just like in the movies which we still called the pictures, and even the flicks; and he stepped on board as the train started its slow glide along the platform, just like in the pictures; and then he found us, and smirked, which rather spoiled the cinematic effect, and smelled his rose and continued to smirk, at least until we had got clear of the railway yards. It was fascinating. This was *la vie en rose*! This, it is to be remembered, at a time when the height of daring was to pull your bike in to a bus stop and chat to a girl; and the height of her daring would be to peel off her gloves and waggle her fingers and then slowly smooth her gloves back on again. Girls were only just beginning to emerge from the chrysalis of their gloves. So kissing like that, in full view – wow! Oblivious of all the friends and all the passengers? Not likely. This clearly was someone who knew his way around.

And so he did. We dozed as best we could, sitting up in the Second Class, and arrived in Melbourne next morning just after the rush hour, and of course it was raining. There was a whole day to fill in before catching the next night train to Sydney. Everyone went their different ways, some possibly to ogle famous Chloe. But he had a better and bohemian idea; no such banalities for him. He knew of a very good record shop and would I like to accompany him? How impressive was that! How marvellous to be so naturally *outré*. He did not call into question the limitation of being Adelaide-based, he comfortably stepped from one place to another. He had already found the answer to the modern postcolonial preoccupation with otherness: he exploited it.

The tired rose was left behind with all the other litter. We found our way somewhere up towards I think maybe the top end of Londsdale Street. The footpaths were wet, the clouds were low, the street noises were more of an exhibition than in Adelaide. In Rundle Street you were so close to the great smooth rubber tyres of the trolley buses that you could just about touch them. The Melbourne streetscapes were grander, and everything happened at a distance, as on a stage. Melbourne is designed for you to be a spectator. But in early winter, it can be very gloomy, Whistleresque. Even the stone buildings seem to eat up the light. Spectacle without visibility. At least, that is how it impressed me at first sighting. Unilluminating. And where was all that famed 'class'? Most of the respectable women had gloves and hats, but that represented a propriety quite familiar to us. The intended grandeur of the city was not as grand as its aspirations, but on the other hand it had an architectural style which was only faintly echoed in Adelaide's civic and business buildings. It felt as though some parts of London might look like that – though whether that was a good thing or not did not occur as a thought. It indicated difference in the same direction as the idea of London indicated difference. If the dull light was oppressive, my horizons were already beginning to shift.

The stubborn persistence of the mizzling rain was more

of a nuisance than the actual dampness. And Melbourne seemed to have given up on verandahs – there was no protection for pedestrians. So it was a relief to wheel in off the street into the record shop. And there he asked about a recently released recording of *La Bohème* (of course!), featuring a new young singer, Marilyn Horne, who had been making a name for herself in Germany. In point of fact she was just on the eve of her triumphant return to the United States, which, incidentally, suggests that America was just as culturally uncertain as Australia; its artists too had to establish themselves abroad to be received at home. He was making some kind of oblique statement in this request: could he listen to it please? This was the sort of store which needed to show it was up to the mark. But of course. The young man serving us had the necessary *hauteur*, the sort of snootiness you wouldn't find in Adelaide, in Allen's for example; but he didn't have just that information at his fingertips ... and of course he didn't have the record in stock. It was much too recent for the antipodes. Melbourne stood exposed as provincial too. The manager was called in and offered us an alternative we didn't know about, a new recording by Eileen Farrell. We were ushered into a sound booth, and yes we required to listen to all three discs to assure ourselves that this production was just as good as he insisted; and so we removed our damp coats, his much longer than mine, and stretched on the deep carpet that all the best record shops used to have, and listened to opera for nearly three hours as a way of escaping the *ennui* of Melbourne. I suppose he listened intently. Perhaps he began to regret the rose, though he did not strike me as sentimental. That way lies a bourgeois idea of bohemianism, and he was playing it to the hilt. More likely, he was thinking of Germany. Which, by implication, is different from lying on your back and thinking of England. Altogether another kind of otherness.

This vignette leads nowhere. There was a conversation with the salesman, carried off with some aplomb. *Hauteur* was now all on our side of the counter. It was a very fine recording, thank you, but expensive, and he would have to reflect on it, to consider whether it was altogether an acceptable substitute, and whether he wanted to pay that much (not much less than a week's wages, come to think of it) for what wasn't his original request, and so on and so on; and we escaped, warmer and dryer than we had entered. And once outside, bursts of scoffing laughter. Eileen Farrell? Married to a policeman? How petit bourgeois was that! We were so smart. Adelaide one; Melbourne nil.

At some stage we must all have gathered together again, and got on the Sydney train, and that meant getting off the train at Albury and on to another one – at least South Australia and Victoria had sorted out that difference. It was confirmation, in a way, that New South Wales really was a separatist state, that it just didn't have anything in common with anyone else. Maybe we slept more on the Sydney train, even in the Second Class, given we had sat up the preceding night; I don't remember. We travelled through the night, and through the next day; sometimes there were flattish paddocks with great granite boulders, and other times there was just the side of a cutting whizzing past, and sometimes there were rolling hills. There were stops and jolting starts in the middle of nowhere, like any train trip to anywhere. And lots of views of backyards, especially as we approached Sydney.

Whatever unimportant detail might have been recalled from this passage through a new part of the world paled by comparison with the instant impact of Sydney itself. If

Melbourne set itself up as some kind of stage, Sydney was all theatre. The backyards were a kind of sneak preview, a tit-illating provocation. Late afternoon, the shadows length-ening, windows lit up and curtains not yet drawn: you never knew just what you might see, and you didn't blink for a moment. Life was on offer, somehow, though there was in fact little enough of it to be seen. Kids coming round the side of a house on their bikes, someone chopping wood, occasionally someone moving about in their kitchen. People not actually caring whether we were looking or not. And that is how it was when we drew into Central Station.

Right from the start, you could see this was a much busier place than any you had experienced before. People were milling about everywhere, stepping in front of each other, wheeling prams or trolleys, making way but keeping on going. There seemed to be no pattern other than movement itself – the worst thing to do was to stop. Which of course is what we did every few steps, to gawk at some new sight, look for some new direction. Everything and everyone was on display. Shockingly, Sydney girls – or at least those who caught suburban trains – wore slacks and short sleeves: that would never do in Adelaide. Nor in Melbourne. Not a pair of gloves in sight. There were barrows of fruit, great mounds of these, and flowers, great buckets of these; the main concourse was a snatch and grab marketplace. This was a place to help yourself, and be quick about it; not a place where anyone offered help. In Adelaide, 'get on with you' was an expression of disbelief. It expressed a comfortable settling down for a yarn. Not here. In Sydney, apparently, it would mean something more like 'move'.

We found the taxi rank and thought ourselves clever in doing so. Taxi ranks were not so easily come by in Adelaide;

you had to know where to look. We didn't at that time realise that you couldn't get out of the station precinct without crossing cordon after cordon of taxis. Down in Belmore Park groups of people seemed to be gathering in the deepening darkness under the trees. They looked somewhat unsteady, but we were familiar with the immediate consequence of six o'clock closing, if that is what still persisted in Sydney. The city was starting to show a disposition to unsteadiness. The taxi dodged through various streets and suddenly we were at the lights near St Mary's spireless Cathedral ('tells you how pointless it is' said the cabbie) and a great squabble was going on between two women opposite the Museum, a squabble that quickly escalated to shrieking and shrill abuse. Should we be stopping to help? It sounded like someone could do with help. But the cabbie wasn't wasting time, he had somewhere else to go. 'Know what that's about?' he asked, 'a new sheila has moved in on someone else's beat.' It took a moment to register. Phwoarrrh. This Sydney! And an established beat that near to the cathedral! Wow. This is why our mothers had been anxious about us going interstate. And we hadn't even got to King's Cross yet.

King's Cross was too much to take in immediately. There were fluorescent lights trying to excite up business, the famous 'Pink Pussycat' at the top of William Street – and the trade was out on each corner of William Street. But we were chiefly anxious to reach our hotel, establish our base. Those other attractions were to be deferred. When we got there, though, we found there had been a mix-up in the arrangements and the hotel was not expecting us for another day. Some of us could be accommodated, but the rest of us were taken to somewhere in the western suburbs to doss down in someone's house for the night. Something like that. Confusion is only a problem for those who expect orderliness. Nobody seemed much fussed, everything just moved along.

And so another vignette. You couldn't organise the experience of Sydney into any tidy narrative pattern. Or rather, it didn't fit any of the patterns we had been given, it didn't fit our preparation. Or possibly, our preparation wasn't well suited to it. There was a disjunction which we had to manage as best we could, and as quickly as we could. We were taken to a place where they said football, meaning soccer. The house was a surprise in many ways. It was a timber and asbestos house. We knew brick, and sometimes stone. You couldn't afford timber in South Australia and, besides, the white ants would eat you out of house and home. This wasn't just a plain house, it was an ugly house. It had no garden. It had no verandah, it had no eaves, it had squinchy little windows. It wasn't sewered: it had an outside dunny. ('This is Sydney?') It was just the bare bones of a house. But it had a room full of records, most of them classical. A surreptitious look: no Marilyn Horne. So I had my chance when mein host, the father of whoever was organising all this, catching me working my way through the titles, politely started a conversation about music. He was, as we used to say, a New Australian, and he had not only a stack of records but an accent, and a stiffish, overly insistent manner, to go with them. He could have got a job in Melbourne, easy. Had he heard of this young American making a name for herself in Germany? No? A pity; but I could recommend a substitute, Eileen Farrell ... He invited me to select something I might like to listen to. It was an awful realisation, that whatever I chose was going to sum me up, expose me. The Melbourne victory was not transferable. Instant revelation upon revelation. All the others were outside getting stuck into snags and beer and having a raucously good time, and here was I trapped in a room of classical records, setting myself apart from everyone else, or so it must have seemed, showing the wrong interests. It was somehow un-Australian; it was like being, well, like being a New Australian perhaps. I was feeling intimidated by the polite, heavily middle-European accent. Or was that a heavily polite accent? Was he being ironic? I know so now. I said the first thing that came into my head. 'You would like Mozart? Of course – but what? Eine kleine ... I would have guessed it.'

The etiquette for this sort of situation eluded me. The world of record playing was still very new to me. How should you look when listening in front of a witness? I sat perched on the arm of a chair, anchored to the player, and listened carefully to every note. I was on my own, even before he presently went away. It was like the process of listening to the whole three discs of an opera you didn't understand – you just had to wait it out until the end, to show that you were appreciating it all. Besides, I didn't know how to stop the machinery, how to get off. I just knew that everyone else was having all the fun.

The fat lady didn't get to sing. Back in the Cross, the streets around our hotel, once we got to it, were singing. There were neon lights everywhere, in fairground pinks and blues. There were strident hustlers and boisterous shopkeepers, and a gauntlet of beggars, and wheels and tyres and trams and buses, a great whirring wash of unceasing clack and clatter. From every doorway and every shop – quite different entrances, we quickly conjectured – came the sounds of Acker Bilk's 'Stranger on the Shore'. And we were a squad of raw johnnies gawping at the big city lights. We were slow to catch on to the underside of all this. The girls standing about were silent, and intimidating to look at. Should you look? The carnivalesque lighting only carried so far: there were dark corners under the verandahs, dark entrances, dark laneways. Even Acker Bilk's clarinet found the loneliness inside the exoticism of his melody. The misery stick, they sometimes called it. We walked past the theatre where Les Girls played, only it wasn't open. King's Cross was sultry, and yet without a charm that caught you up; rather, one that arrested you momentarily.

This was the Cross before Vietnam, before American R and R dollars spoiled everything. No doubt both dollars and GIs had made their way to the Cross during the Second World War, but it had survived that campaign fairly unscathed. There weren't hamburger places cheek by jowl up Darlinghurst Road. Nor was there yet an El Alamein fountain, just a rather scruffy little park where all sorts of flotsam and jetsam, human and other kinds of debris, drifted into the corners. The Cross was still largely connected to its past. Indeed, in some ways it had a stronger connection with the past than just about anywhere else. The characters round about were, as journalists say, colourful. In fact they gave the effect of no colour at all, just grubby. But the idea of them was colourful. Somewhere Rosaleen Norton, whom we had read about in *Pix* and *Truth* and the *Mirror* and other such publications, was no doubt practising her witchcraft (another dark, colourful business) on orchestral conductors and, for all we knew, tram conductors too. What we encountered was both more visible and invisible.

Sitting in the café beneath the 'Pink Pussycat', day after day, was a woman of indeterminate age, angry-looking, with boiled popping eyes and thin straight greasy hair, and a perfectly round head. Her clothes were soiled and didn't fit anywhere, and it was difficult to decide whether she or they were shapeless. Sometimes she rummaged around in a big bag leaning against her leg, tumbling over strangely-shaped packages, like travelling with her own unlucky dip. How could you not stare? From time to time she hectored the passing world in a loud hoarse voice; not that the passing world paid heed. It did not even notice her. She could have been the mother of Albert, the magic pudding. She could have stepped straight out of the pages of Dickens. If she was not the representative archetype of the Cross, she certainly epitomised some key element of it.

It was that residual Dickensian effect that so caught the eye, and the imagination – Dickensian dark lanes and alleys, Dickensian gloom under the canopies of the shop fronts, the same litter and noise and compressed range of humanity. The characters here were all slightly exaggerated, sitting too noticeably on doorsteps, guttersnipes shouting cheek at shopkeepers, people taking up too much room and nattering too loudly in front of the shops, at street corners, careless whether they were impeding anyone else, much like today's mobile phone users only you could see the other party. They all seemed to carry a patina of tawdriness, they were all slightly dated. It was seedy, but it was interesting. They all knew each other; there was the kind of vitality expressed that would never do in a polite and proper community, concerned with presenting as respectable. Somehow, what was written in books connected with what you could see and feel in a life lived on the streets. You could see why art would imitate life here; there was plenty to write about. Adelaide wasn't like that; and if Adelaide had been written about at all, it wasn't where you would easily find it. Privately, you suspected it might not be much of a read anyway. Which possibly means that Oscar Wilde's inversion didn't apply there, or perhaps that Adelaide was not quite ready for him.

Just down from the Pink Pussycat was one of the notorious streets we had heard whispered about even in Adelaide. Palmer Street wasn't what we had imagined, though who can tell what we were imagining? We had wheeled off into the sidestreets, still bunched together for something like moral support, in case that was needed. Here the terrace houses were amazing to us: they were built right on to the street front. And more amazing still, people left their front door wide open. Anyone could walk in ... such poignant innocence. We were still opening our eyes. Occasionally you could see people moving around down in the light at the far end of a narrow passage. Life, such as it might be, was on offer again. The late afternoon sun showed mellow tints in the sandstone walls, though mostly there was a thick layer of street grime. At a cross street, though, spectacle had come right out into the open: the local children had wrenched palings from various fences, found pieces of packing cases and dead branches, and they had started a bonfire. And soon enough bungers were going off, and people were starting to drift together right in the middle of the intersection, and who knows, maybe the asphalt was starting to bubble away under the embers. More distant explosions could be heard from streets near by, and sometimes the echoes bounced off the sides of buildings, making a sound like distant artillery. This was cracker night, at the wrong time of the year. Empire Day or some such, not Guy Fawkes Day.

Once again New South Wales had put itself out of step and was careless of it. If a named day was to be celebrated, to commemorate a distant but historically colourful event, why would you be so cavalier about it? Adelaide's Guy Fawkes Day belonged in the suburbs, in the backyards or in vacant lots we still called paddocks. At an early age I had been wheeled around the streets in a pram, dressed in my father's gardening clothes and holding a tin pannikin, a guy collecting pennies for our fireworks. In that first week in November we made a bonfire of all the garden refuse and burned all the accumulated litter, the vine cuttings and bits pruned from the fruit trees, the tatters of the previous year's sweetcorn and sweetpeas, dried pumpkin runners and whatever vegetables – potatoes, tomatoes, beans – had been replaced with new plantings. Guy Fawkes wasn't just about letting off crackers, shooting rockets over the roof ridge, or getting dark grey powder on your clothes, in your hair, sometimes in your eye. Or checking the streets the next morning for unexploded squibs. It was also about cleaning out the last of the dead midyear, and the potatoes we baked in the ashes could I suppose be read as some kind of secular sacrament, though such a strongly non-conformist community as ours didn't set much store by formal ritual. But we did know when we had our hands on an historical tradition. There were few enough of these and we weren't going to surrender them readily. What Sydney had done was wilful negligence – either that, or a kind of swanking that didn't impress. On the other hand, we had a sneaking admiration for the bare-faced cheek of setting light to an intersection. We would never have got away with that back home. Nor would we have got away with using the language of some of the children eddying round the fire, the light of the flames catching their faces, the smoke curling and settling above them, the deepening darkness of the evening closing in behind them.

A 'social' of some kind had been organised for us – basically, an open bar, something to nibble, some music, and nurses, as many as you could lay your hands on, so to speak.

Phwoarrrh again – nurses! But just what did you do when you encountered a nurse? What kind of clever provocative thing did you say, what could you get away with? Again, there seemed to be an understanding that lots of the others arrived at very quickly, as they disappeared in pairs into the Sydney night, with the suggestion that no one should worry to stay up for them. They had every intention of not returning. The carnal itch was everywhere, and contagious. This Sydney. Good times were promised, the siren city beckoned; and winked.

I do not remember much about the nurse I was introduced to. She was small, she seemed very nice, she was from the country. Which meant in Sydney terms that she may as well have been from out of state. I do remember recognising that there seemed to be a whole set of social skills I was missing, an anxiety about the protocols of whatever was about to happen. Consciousness-raising had yet to become the precursor of political correctness, but it was clearly already in the air, and in the way. On the other hand, the city itself seemed such an interesting place, even or especially after six o'clock, and its soft yellow lighting led you on and on. So we found ourselves walking through the streets, me ever hopeful of some enticing park or garden where we might pause a while. The 'Invercargill March' was also in my head though, with the words I knew, words of an old World War II song I had heard from my uncles: 'Oh the maggots walked up Pitt Street with their boots on ...' Acker Bilk was crowded out for the time being. There were amazing shops selling guns and swords and knives, shops full of all sorts of junk, pawnshops. No doubt these existed in Adelaide, but not anywhere I knew. These were shops that seemed to be museums of curiosities, more interested in accumulating than selling. Somehow we wended our way as far as Belmore Park again, but while the shadows under the trees seemed in advance to be a good prospect, the park turned out fairly densely inhabited, possibly by the same people who had been there previously, and the weaving and wavering figures were too disconcertingly raucous, intrusive, to attempt any temporary dalliance. At the same time, it seemed at least strategic to keep the conversation going – I talked, God how I talked, to keep the distances we were walking from becoming noticeable. And the inevitable outcome of this extended promenade, these would-be night manoeuvres, was that we ended up at the front door of the nurses' quarters, where the tired pencil pines threw a thin shadow over the shallow porch. We had made a traverse right across the length of the city. Some romantic adventure. The poor girl had no doubt been walked off her feet up and down the wards all day ... she couldn't say goodnight quickly enough. Which left me feeling dissatisfied with the way the evening had worked out.

Acker Bilk was still calling the tune back near the hotel.

A dinner-dance on the Harbour, meaning something like a floating barbecue, had been arranged for the interstate visitors. It was too much to hope for that the nurse from the country would be there, though she had led me to think she might come along. But she didn't show up at the Quay at the appointed time. Sydney was not living up to its promise either. This was a long way from *la vie en rose*, or the grand passions of opera. Was there something I didn't know? Well yes, that there was plenty I didn't know. In fact, there were plenty of others similarly crestfallen. The girls of Sydney were either fickle or not easily impressed. We all tromped up the gangway and on to the stubby little yellow and red ferry, and bustled around for the best possie and settled down for the night tour.

One of Sydney's best kept secrets is that you cannot see anything worth seeing on the Harbour in the darkness, especially when the windows are all misted up with too much heavy breathing. You couldn't stand outside as there was no deck to speak of: this was a tubby little vessel, a scrubber of a certain age, jostling in amongst the big ferries on their regular beat. With all these trips, once you leave the Quay, with the city lights behind it, the journey is pretty much into the night; obviously. Truth in advertising ... There are occasional navigation lights, and once or twice an island might loom up; but in early winter it was much too dark to make any sense of where you were in relation to anything else. You could be under the Bridge and not know it; and there was no Opera House then to act as a reference point.

And on these excursions you could not, you still cannot, escape the music. There is after all a limited distance between you and the nearest very loud-speaker. All you can do in such circumstances is go pale, mute and miserable, and wish for deafness. Either that, or drink yourself silly; which didn't seem such an attractive option, given the close-up competition. The heavy drinkers gradually encroached on the limited dancing space, their staggering a sad parody of the dancers. All this is billed as the defining romantic event, yet what it does is induce despair, enforce anti-social thoughts and attitudes. What chance would ardour have in such a venue? The design of the ferry was a row of seats all round the sides, which meant that you had to skew around in your seat, rick your back to peer out through the space you smeared in all the condensation. Everything about it was uncomfortable. The bleakness outside seemed to leak into the cabin area, to leak into your very soul, in poignant contrast to the allure of the city itself; though slowly it was becoming clear that what it really did was emphasise the nature of that allure. The Harbour is a large and serenely indifferent lake: large enough to be, at night, a type of the void, indifferent enough to discover our essential loneliness. Acker Bilk one; visitors nil. Back at the terminal, where the ferry berthed, a lifebuoy hung on a bracket. Too late.

At the end of the week there was a train to catch back to Melbourne. Belmore Park, outside Central Station, looked a lot less sinister in the light of day. Yet it did not wholly relinquish its power to disturb. In the middle of a patch of grass a woman lay sprawled asleep, her grey woollen skirt ruched up over her thighs, one shoe kicked off, her face either bloated or swollen. The workers and shoppers streaming out from the station paid her no heed, they kept on moving along; and she, patently, was oblivious to them. That was Sydney. Lying there, she seemed to combine so many different elements of what I had been observing; evidently, abandonment could mean two very different things at the same time. But the essential difference between a life like this, and that over-wrought in opera, remained elusive. Or was it all just a matter of style?

During the day-long stopover in Melbourne I wandered by myself, for preference, down through the other end of the city, and found an open door, much as in Sydney. This one led into the gallery of the Contemporary Art Group, about which I knew nothing. It sounded as interesting as anything else – and indeed it was. Melbourne seemed to be a place where you stepped aside for a time, and got your cultural fix. It was a répris in little of the whole of the preceding week. It was something I had discovered for myself, without knowing what I would encounter. I went into the low-lit gallery, slightly amateurish in its crowded presentation, and there before me were a range of challenging, even disturbing paintings, unlike any I had seen before; I stepped outside again, and it was the same world, only different. Years later I read of David Campbell's encounter with symboliste paintings in a London exhibition. That had opened up for him a new way of seeing the world, and a new way of writing about it in his poetry. Some much more modest moment on the Damascus road had been mine too, or so I like to think.

The point, if there is one, is just how easily as well as dramatically our impressions can be changed, our way of seeing and knowing rearranged. That was likewise the case on the trip home. The train jounced and rocked and rattled across the Ninety Mile Plains, renamed Coonalpyn Downs if you please, and we dozed fitfully and sometimes slept and were shaken awake when the big Victorian diesel was uncoupled at the Tailem Bend shunting yard or wherever it was. All the impressions of the week were being shaken around and resolving into a new kind of pattern, like a kaleidoscope in reverse. Something had changed, nothing had changed. We returned to Adelaide reassured of our own values; and yet we had observed differences, observed if not fully shared in social patterns that were not our own. Other possibilities existed than those offered us in our own backyard. There were other options. This did not provoke dissatisfaction; after all, we were returning home. What we had sensed was something like enlargement without displacement; it would be too dramatic, too operatic, to think that one week's furlough would radically change one's view of life. On the other hand, several hours in the Contemporary Art Gallery could pretty nearly achieve something like that. We weren't disaffiliated by this encounter with the bigtimers in the East. If anything, we knew our own place all the better.

And that is something they didn't know.

Wakefield Press is an independent publishing and
distribution company based in Adelaide, South Australia.
We love good stories and publish beautiful books.
To see our full range of titles, please visit our website at
www.wakefieldpress.com.au.